AF766739

REIMAGINING POVERTY THROUGH SOCIAL CONTEXTUAL ANALYSES

This book is the first of its kind to apply social contextual analysis to the issue of poverty. It sets out detailed accounts of poverty based on original research and shows how understanding life contexts can give us a deeper understanding of the issue.

The book highlights detailed life contexts from a project exploring the everyday experience of poverty, including what poverty is and what psychology has to say about poverty. It showcases work from an original study in Australia that uses on-the-ground participatory interview research, integrating this with international literature to provide a comprehensive analysis of poverty. The chapters explore the complexity, and often the simplistic reductions used in answering questions that try to define poverty, the psychological understanding of the phenomena, how individuals experience it, and the general opinion of the status-quo regarding poverty. However, most importantly the book tries to investigate why we have not solved poverty in modern, capitalist life, and sets out recommendations for research, practice, and policy in addressing issues of poverty.

Showing the need for rigorous and on-the-ground approaches to addressing poverty and its many complications, the book will be highly relevant to students and researchers in the fields of social psychology, critical psychology, community psychology, social work, and social policy. It will also be relevant for anyone interested in the application of social psychological research techniques to the understanding and intervention of social issues, by showing pathways to better explore and understand human behaviour.

Eden Thain is a research fellow at the Australian Centre for Child Protection, University of South Australia, and a member of the Social Contextual Analysis of Human Behaviour Research Group.

Exploring the Environmental and Social Foundations of Human Behaviour

Series Editor
Bernard Guerin
Professor of Psychology, University of South Australia

Can you imagine that everything people do, say and think is shaped directly by engaging with our many environmental and social contexts? Humans would then really be part of their environment.

For current psychology, however, people only engage with metaphorical 'internal' environments or brains events, and everything we do somehow originates hidden in there. But what if all that we do and think originated out in our worlds, and what we call 'internal' is merely language and conversations which were also shaped by engaging in our external discursive, cultural and societal environments?

Exploring Human Behaviour as Directly Engaged in its Environments is an exciting new book series about developing the next generation of ways to understand what people do, say and think. Human behaviour is shaped through directly engaging in our diverse contexts of resources, social relationships, economics, culture, discourses, colonization, patriarchy, society, and the opportunities afforded by our birth contexts. Even language and thinking arise from our external social and discursive contexts, and so the 'internal' and brain metaphors will disappear as psychology becomes merged with the social sciences.

The series is therefore a-disciplinary and presents analyses or contextually-engaged research on topics which describe or demonstrate how human behaviour arises from direct engagement with the worlds in which we are embedded.

In this series:

Reimagining Therapy through Social Contextual Analyses: *Finding New Ways to Support People in Distress: Volume 7*

Reimagining Poverty through Social Contextual Analyses: *Finding New Ways to Understand 'Getting By': Volume 8*

REIMAGINING POVERTY THROUGH SOCIAL CONTEXTUAL ANALYSES

Finding New Ways to Understand 'Getting By'

Eden Thain

Routledge
Taylor & Francis Group
LONDON AND NEW YORK

Designed Cover image: © Shutterstock

First published 2024
by Routledge
4 Park Square, Milton Park, Abingdon, Oxon OX14 4RN

and by Routledge
605 Third Avenue, New York, NY 10158

Routledge is an imprint of the Taylor & Francis Group, an informa business

© 2024 Eden Thain

The right of Eden Thain to be identified as author of this work has been asserted in accordance with sections 77 and 78 of the Copyright, Designs and Patents Act 1988.

All rights reserved. No part of this book may be reprinted or reproduced or utilised in any form or by any electronic, mechanical, or other means, now known or hereafter invented, including photocopying and recording, or in any information storage or retrieval system, without permission in writing from the publishers.

Trademark notice: Product or corporate names may be trademarks or registered trademarks, and are used only for identification and explanation without intent to infringe.

British Library Cataloguing-in-Publication Data
A catalogue record for this book is available from the British Library

Library of Congress Cataloging-in-Publication Data
Names: Thain, Eden, author.
Title: Reimagining poverty through social contextual analyses :
finding new ways to understand "getting by" / Eden Thain.
Description: New York, NY : Routledge, 2024. |
Series: Exploring the environmental and social foundations of human behaviour |
Includes bibliographical references and index.
Identifiers: LCCN 2023050280 (print) | LCCN 2023050281 (ebook) |
ISBN 9781032592817 (hardback) | ISBN 9781032592756 (paperback) |
ISBN 9781003453970 (ebook)
Subjects: LCSH: Poverty. | Poverty–Psychological aspects. |
Behaviorism (Psychology) | Human behavior. | Social psychology.
Classification: LCC HC79.P6 T463 2024 (print) |
LCC HC79.P6 (ebook) | DDC 339.4/6–dc23/eng/20240105
LC record available at https://lccn.loc.gov/2023050280
LC ebook record available at https://lccn.loc.gov/2023050281

ISBN: 9781032592817 (hbk)
ISBN: 9781032592756 (pbk)
ISBN: 9781003453970 (ebk)

DOI: 10.4324/9781003453970

Typeset in Optima
by Newgen Publishing UK

CONTENTS

List of Figures *vi*
List of Tables *vii*
Preface *ix*
Acknowledgements *xi*
A Note on the Terms Used in This Book *xiii*

1 How to Help Those in Poverty 1

2 What Is Poverty? 11

3 Psychology of Poverty 33

4 The Contexts of Poverty 48

5 The Experiences of Poverty 70

6 Pathways in Poverty 97

7 Discourses in Poverty 119

8 Why We Have Not Solved Poverty 144

Index *152*

FIGURES

2.1 The basic process of our lives with money 12
5.1 The social contextual cycle of getting by 93
6.1 Teresa's pathways in poverty 98
6.2 Natalie's pathways in poverty 108
7.1 Neoliberal and solidarity discourses and the balancing act 125

TABLES

2.1	Types of Poverty Described with Example Measures	16
2.2	Concepts of Poverty with a Comparison of Concept Qualities	27
4.1	Shared Contexts in Australian Qualitative Research with 'The Poor'	53
5.1	Participant Demographics	75
5.2	Interconnection Examples from Participant Talk	86
5.3	Catch-22's of Constraints Experienced by Participants	87
5.4	Important Social Relationships Mentioned by Participants	89
7.1	Repertoires of the Neoliberal Discourse from Data	128
7.2	Repertoires for the Solidarity Discourse from Data	134

PREFACE

This book uses social contextual analysis to ask the questions: what is poverty and why aren't we fixing it? The concept of poverty is both complex and complicated. Often in everyday life and psychology research, it is simplified to a problematic degree. The simplicity ignores life contexts and misattributes the 'cause' of poverty to poor people or rather something 'internal' to their psychology. Putting the contexts of life back into the analysis produces a forward-looking approach to poverty that should interest researchers and clinicians who must grapple with these economic realities for people they work with in nations like Australia.

To complete this work I reviewed poverty definitions, the 'psychology of poverty', and qualitative investigations of poverty. But, to bring back the contexts in psychological understandings of poverty, I decided to go out and see as much of everyday poverty as I could. In this book, I present those findings but focus on my first-hand experiences researching using participatory and conversational methods with a community group and nine cases of people experiencing poverty.

I will show you that reducing complexity is potentially the source of even more issues for those suffering in poverty. Throughout psychology and other social sciences, the need to homogenise 'the poor' accompanies a focus on deficits without the complex relational realities of poverty. The simplification removes avenues of intervention from consideration and creates divisions between 'real poor' and other groups that are equally suffering. This separation seems to benefit no one.

Despite complexity there may be more direct solutions for poverty. Importantly, as I wrote this book to show what I learnt as a psychology PhD student, the most impactful thing I walked away with is without more information on contextual pathways in poverty psychological researchers and clinicians may be unable to assist with stressors in the lives of poor people using our mainstream internally focused paradigm. Possible solutions arise through a more thoughtful understanding of resources and relationships in context. That understanding will move psychology from its individualist focus toward a social science as it needs to be.

ACKNOWLEDGEMENTS

I want to thank many people for making this possible.

First and foremost, Bernard Guerin, for supporting this work and my continuing development as an academic and professional. Many elements of this research were brought to life by his knowledge and guidance. Bernard has also kept me out of poverty by being a key relationship for my economic survival – thank you!

I must thank my family, Tyler, and Leopold. I want to work to support you, and since this research has finished, I hope I have been able to give the focus needed back to our family despite still working so much.

There are many colleagues and friends that kept both my research and my life going through these years. Some helped by giving me some of the most basic tools and concepts needed even to begin projects like this one, while some were there as a helping hand, and others improved my time just by their conversation and companionship. Others have given me confidence and inspired me to continue forward with teaching and learning by allowing me to be the one they turn to for advice and guidance.

And, of course, I would like to thank everyone I worked with in my years researching for this book. I owe everything I know in the following pages to the participants, informants, and helpful colleagues in the area. My participants shared their lives with me, and I have been able to take them on and learn and teach others what I have learned. I wish I could name everyone who has dedicated so much time and effort to sharing with me, working with me, and just getting to know me; you have taught me about yourselves and inspired my passion for change. Since my research concluded, my life has been a whirlwind of change, but I know what I learned in this research helped me become who I need to be. I hope what little I helped with in these years has been useful and inspiring as you were to me.

I hope to always stand in solidarity against the challenges of poverty.

A NOTE ON THE TERMS USED IN THIS BOOK

I use "poverty" and "the poor" to refer to the people and contexts I researched with and am trying to describe. Dehumanising and distant language like this is viewed, rightfully, as pejorative and derogatory. Initially, in recruitment materials and first drafts, I did not use these phrases. My professional training told me it was ethical to avoid those terms, that it would open my research to many more people that were poor but did not identify with the label. Then, with the people I was – apparently – protecting with my language choices, my participants and informants confronted me for avoiding the term "the poor". They took it on as their truth, just as much to confirm that horrid things were said about them but then to challenge those connotations, bring attention to the need to humanise those less fortunate, and foster solidarity. My avoidance of saying 'poor' or 'poverty' was professional pandering; "I'm poor! Say it!". I was avoiding the bad things participants lived with for my ethical protection.

I reflected on my own life; I found that I considered myself as someone who was, and had been, "struggling" but never as someone who was "poor". I was creating a separate group that was *really* in trouble, but I had no solidarity with. Like my participants now I want to be a poor person speaking about poverty – though I am hardly in poverty anymore. The later chapters on discourse argue that poverty is not a singular phenomenon but socially–contextually bound through interaction. My use of these terms hopefully highlights the discomfort, gets you to sit with it, helps you recognise the lack of uniformity in the experience, and reflects on the solidarity needed between all those struggling to get by.

All participant names are pseudonyms and some identifying details have been altered as needed without altering the essence of the points made.

1

HOW TO HELP THOSE IN POVERTY

I could take you through the arguments of previous research, cases of real people, and theories for change in poverty but most people already know the quickest way to help those suffering in poverty:

Give people more money

That is a crux of poverty. That the world revolves around being able to buy what you need from others, and to sell your labour, knowledge, skills, or other resources to get money to keep that process going. This is the core idea of poverty in the media, in government policy, in academic psychology and everyday knowledge.

> There's an alternative theory of poverty that some of us have been trying to get across, which is that it's not a character flaw – it is a lack of money.
>
> *(Ehrenreich, 2006)*

And after all:

> There is no particular reason to count the poor unless you are going to do something about them.
>
> *(Orshansky, 1969, p. 37)*

Not only is this self-evident from how the global economy works in the 21st century, but we also have evidence from unconditional cash transfer and universal basic income (UBI) research to back up this direct solution. Giving people free cash:

DOI: 10.4324/9781003453970-1

- Reduces stress (UK: Johnson & Johnson, 2019; Kangas et al., 2019)
- Improves mental health (Review: Wilson & McDaid, 2021; New York City: Kumar et al., 2023)
- Improves health outcomes (Review: Gibson et al., 2018)
- Provides a way out of 'the poverty trap' (Bangladesh: Balboni et al., 2022*)

*It is important to note this book largely focuses only on the Economic Global North/West/Liberal Residual Welfare States, so comparison to outcomes elsewhere is limited.

A UBI has also been suggested as a solution to the trauma currently being brought about by the devastating economic shocks of COVID-19 (Johnson et al., 2020). Support for such intervention is growing, alongside wealth inequality – including some of the UK public believing a UBI would be more effective than medication for reducing distress (Bridger & Nettle, 2022). Otherwise, cash transfer research has produced null results, which have a variety of explanations, largely methodological (see Jacob et al., 2022). There is simply no good argument against providing cash provisions to those struggling in poverty.

We have other psychological basics to consider. In Australia, our welfare provision is largely residual benefits for unemployment and disability (unemployment payments are called Jobseeker, though throughout the research period for this book's content it was called NewStart). Those benefits are run through the system of 'mutual obligations'. Put simply, to keep getting this benefit unemployed people must complete obligations including but not limited to:

- Agreeing to a 'Job Plan'
  (the set of obligations)
- Regular appointments with an employment service provider
  (private companies that monitor if obligations are met)
- Go-to job interviews
- Work part-time
- Apply for jobs (e.g., 20 a month)
- Go to provided training
  (can be formal or informal education)
- 'Work for the dole': a community job
- Accept work 'deemed suitable'
- Do voluntary work

All of these to gain $346.05 a week paid fortnightly as of early 2023, which is $269 below the poverty line (Davidson et al., 2023). Nearly half of the people required to complete these activities are noted to have a limited capacity to work (40%+; DSS, 2022). Ultimately, recipients are held under threat that if they do not keep up their end of the obligation, they will lose their payment and they do lose their payment; according to the Department of Social Security's data, during data collection for the research in this book between July 2017 and June 2018 in Australia 1,920,298 jobseekers were reported for non-attendance – potentially triggering a payment suspension – with 25.5% non-attending for a valid reason (DEWR, 2018). It has been otherwise documented how those that are 'breached' (payment suspended) are sometimes for reasons that seem unconscionable (see Casey, 2017). Surviving already has its difficulties – everyone is anxious about their next paycheck – but being in receipt of government benefits comes with so much more monitoring and punishment.

The calls to 'Raise the Rate' of Australia's unemployment benefit, in its current context, reach back over a decade (Henry et al., 2010) and the rate has not been lifted in real terms, above inflation, since 1994 (though during COVID-19 a boost was implemented). In 2023, a survey of 1609 people by Resolve Political Monitor found that 43% of those polled supported a raise to JobSeeker with 26% undecided (Galloway, 2023). So, we have community recognition of the inadequacy of the payment.

There is some psych 101 to apply here. The aim of this system is to increase behaviour in the job market. If we want people to increase behaviour, should we punish or reinforce actions related to the target outcome? Everything you could learn in an initial psychology class will tell you that you should reinforce the behaviours related to the target, and that punishment reduces behaviour frequency. Punish someone too much and they will learn helplessness. For some reason, these basic lessons, still taught in psych 101, and foundational to some of our basic learning theories, are not heeded. Someone trying to get to 20 job applications a month but missing out will not be rewarded for the work they have done but punished for not reaching the target. Such punishment, theoretically, will result in dropping out of the labour market and obligation system more than it should encourage that person to apply for more and get that job.

The effort put in gets recipients an amount of money lower than the poverty line: not much of a reward. We will discuss in Chapter 2 the outcomes of not having enough money, but put simply it's not enough food, not enough social engagement, and poor mental health. All more roadblocks to the positive fruitful behaviour in the community the system intends, and ultimately the doubling down on obligations, is just another punishment.

So, how do we know more money would help and is supported by both basic psychological theory and scientific evidence but somehow never happens? There are some common objections:

1 People will use free money poorly.
2 It will lead people to be lazy.

3 It will destroy the economy.
4 They don't deserve it.

There are arguments against all these worries; I will give some points below but rather than make armchair arguments, we will move to real research throughout this book with people's lived experiences. That does not change the core issue – money gets resources needed to live well and poor people do not have access to money or these resources.

First, poor people use money poorly. This generally is true, but everyone is bad at money. Research suggests that you probably have poor financial literacy (Adamkovič & Martončik, 2017; Wolf, 2018), you are 'innately irrational' – or at least have bounded rationality – which is why you will make 'bad' choices (Ariely, 2008; Kahneman, 2003; Simon, 1972; Sunstein, 2017; Zafirovski, 2005), and you will usually make choices that seem hedonistic or for gratification (Adamkovič & Martončik, 2017). It is only when we speak about the poor and their limited funds that suddenly this human-wide set of normal traits becomes a moral ill. People make 'bad' choices because some of them are the bread and butter of life, and some are fun and loving bad choices because our goal is not economic or mathematical rationality – but getting by with each other.

Will the poor become lazy and directionless with nothing to contribute? We do not know. There are no solid data sets on what happens when we give everyone big unconditional cash transfers. But for some reason, at least in Australia, you are allowed to claim repeatedly "The best form of welfare is a job" (see Australian HANSARD – too many politicians to reference). Similarly in academic arenas the issue of poverty has been reduced to work effort (P. R. Saunders, 2004). The other possibility exists as suggested by cash transfer research, that people are happier and healthier, and theoretically being happy and healthy will break a constant feedback loop the poor are stuck in (Haushofer & Fehr, 2014). The 'job first' mentality is not working, so we could try this new promising angle and see if everyone gets lazy, then we can work on that.

The economy will be destroyed if we just give money to those with the least. From arguments about inflation to the above issue of work ethic, people have made benevolent cash transfers seem like a destructive force. The simple fact is poor people will be spending money mostly on essentials. If you cannot afford rent and a meal, then it is most likely you would spend that new money on those things. This is where the above 'bad choices' argument comes back where poor people may go pay for a pub meal rather than cook at home – but that is money into the economy. Deloitte's economic projections during this research indicated a $4 billion 'prosperity dividend' which would likely create jobs (2018). The logic seems clear: poor people finally can go eat out (they do), the places have new and more customers and then need more staff to serve them. Such demand-side injections are not revelatory – see the Australian Labour Government's 2009 stimulus (Murphy, 2017).

Finally, who deserves help? Deserving is an interesting construct, best addressed with the relational nature of making money. Most poverty is considered a personal issue without other people. But all economics is founded on exchange (Polanyi, 1944/2001; Simmel, 1907/1971). There is a giver and a receiver. We exist in networks. We get things through others. To analyse poverty, we must analyse the steps resources take through people – the full context. We need to remember that being poor makes others treat you in certain ways; pain you are expected to live through mental and physical (Summers et al., 2021).

Unfortunately, in Australia many could be classified as 'poor'. During my research (2018), 13.6% of Australia's population was living in income poverty (Davidson et al., 2020, p. 9). Remember though, that statistic is presented in an easy to digest format with all the complicating and contextual elements removed. But the contextual experience of poverty as it really happens is much less clear cut. So, in the following chapters, I will try to bring back the contextual intersections, interactions, and everyday behaviours for getting by. At the same time, I want to present a critique of the history of 'the psychology of poverty' and psychology's distance from economics (Carr & Sloan, 2003, p. 163; Guerin, 2003, p. 698; 2016, p. 86; Lea et al., 1987, p. xix; Rachlin, 1980, p. 212). Because today, we all know, very little of human behaviour is free of economics (Guerin, 2016, 2020).

Reflexive Note

Let's start with what I have done: what my project was. I am going to try to tell you what I learned during my PhD. I conducted reviews asking the questions: What is poverty? What does psychology say about poverty? And what is poverty like? The first few chapters will summarise what the academic body of work answers these questions with. The following chapters are about my own research, I went out and I collected my own data.

My project was an exercise in Conversational Research (Guerin et al., 2018). My data collection began in December 2016 and ended in February 2019. Between January 2017 and the end of 2018, I carried out multi-hour recorded interviews, the core data I am drawing on now. I recruited nine people of different genders and ages who self-identified as being on low incomes or receiving welfare. I posted online and handed out flyers while I participated in a political and support Community Group which was 'By the poor for the poor'. With 2–7 interviews per participant, I completed 30 formal interviews between an hour and three and half hours, averaging 2.5 hours per interview, for 70 hours of recorded conversations. We discussed anything participants considered related to their lives in poverty.

I also participated in over 30 community events for 120+ hours of participation for which I wrote field notes. My participation included public events, driving members and equipment around, attending organisational meetings, and taking minutes (I was always noting anyway). I also participated in political agitation at government meetings, NGO meetings, and meetings with politicians. I participated in efforts to spread information, I assisted in the efforts of the people's organisations, and I helped with general group maintenance, including handing out flyers, group lunches, and spaces for the community to meet. I was also an online member in social media spaces. My analysis draws largely on interview data, but my learning from all avenues is entangled throughout this book.

The interview participants were compensated for their time with a $50 gift card. And the whole research was supported by the Australian government's Research Training Program (RTP) – PhD scholarship.

Who Am I?

As a young person, I had my own experiences in poverty and with welfare systems. When I was very young my family had two incomes, comfortably middle class in a metropolitan Australian city, at the age of 12 through family breakdown I began to receive my own welfare payment called Youth Allowance – for supporting my studies. Initially $75 a fortnight – most of this went to a phone bill every month otherwise to my dinner, often a frozen pizza. As the amount increased, I moved out of home at 17, I continued Youth Allowance and eventually moved to Newstart (unemployment benefits). Throughout all this time I was studying, but welfare was my core income, how I got-by. The amount ranged from $120 to $250 a fortnight, most of it going to rent and bills. From 16 to 22 I was underweight and lived simply. I had my encounters with welfare agencies, being yelled at over a desk for being a cheat (they had stuffed up some paperwork on their end). It was not until I started this PhD that I started to earn money that gave me more freedom. I studied and worked as I could but I was going to 'make it', and I guess I did. I got into and completed a PhD. I can only imagine what I could have achieved with more money, more food, more freedom to socialise.

I came into this research to learn about others, but I now understand my own experiences more. Through interviews, I disclosed my experiences, and this encouraged participants to share:

> Well, it's only natural that you are going to add to some idea, to some degree, some of yourself to it because it's your life as well. You have lived

this as well. It's only natural that you are going to need to add a layer of yourself.

Participant – Sandra

So, I was an insider. On the other hand, in the community group context, I was and tried to remain an outsider. Using a term of Alder and Alder (1987), I was an 'active member', part of the main activities but not fully committing to the values and goals of the group – though I do wholeheartedly share them. Taking an active member position limited my influence on the group's inner workings and stopped my educational status from being something that swayed opinions. This hands-off, low-impact observation and interviewing seemed to work, as my participant Natalie remarked close to the end of the data collection period, "I forget you're there, like a little fixture, observing".

Being an insider was not solely a benefit and even created some issues. For example, some participants expected me to have personal knowledge of many of their experiences. When this happened, participants passed over explaining details of their story; I then had to ask them to share their experiences in detail directly. All participants were immediately receptive to this point, but it is a pitfall of being an insider.

My exit from the group also bares note. In the time immediately following the end of this research, I underwent major changes in my life – I was a young man with a partner and consistent work as a PhD student when I started the study. As I write this, I am an out and proud trans woman and a parent. My PhD ended as the COVID-19 pandemic began, just as I was finalising corrections on my thesis, and my job prospects shifted. With a new child, my economic worries, and my transition, part of my coping was to close large elements of my life including this participation. I am attempting to rekindle the connections to this work through this book.

Conclusion

Altogether, this is me, this is what I have done, and these things are what I would like to tell you about. Both as someone that went through this and as someone that is trying to remember that everyone has a unique context, and a unique path through and about poverty. I hope I can capture and show you that complexity.

This book's core message is a contrast between academic understandings of poverty and how poverty appears in the everyday experience of the poor. Frankly, when I tried to learn what poverty was, I found the academic literature not only difficult to read but also more confusing as someone who had lived on welfare and gone hungry. The focus on money seemed particularly silly. Of course, it is key, but it is not really what I cared about.

But that brings me to my first question: what is poverty?

References

Adamkovič, M., & Martončik, M. (2017). A review of consequences of poverty on economic decision-making: A hypothesized model of a cognitive mechanism. *Frontiers in Psychology, 8*, 1784. https://doi.org/10.3389/fpsyg.2017.01784

Adler, P. A., & Adler, P. (1987). *Membership roles in field research*. Sage Publications, Inc.

Ariely, D. (2008) *Predictably irrational*. Harper Collins.

Balboni, C., Bandiera, O., Burgess, R., Ghatak, M., & Heil, A. (2022) Why do people stay poor? *The Quarterly Journal of Economics, 137*(2), 785–844. https://doi.org/10.1093/qje/qjab045

Bridger, E., & Nettle, D. (2022). Public perceptions of the effectiveness of income provision on reducing psychological distress. *Journal of Public Mental Health, 21*(3), 208–217. https://doi.org/10.1108/JPMH-04-2022-0036

Carr, S., & Sloan, T. (Eds.). (2003). *Poverty and psychology: From global perspective to local practice*. Springer Science & Business Media.

Casey, S. (2017). *Resistance in employment services: A critical account*. RMIT University. https://researchrepository.rmit.edu.au/esploro/outputs/doctoral/Resistance-in-employment-services-a-critical/9921863895201341#file-0

Davidson, P., Bradbury, B., & Wong, M. (2023). *Poverty in Australia 2023: Who is affected Poverty and Inequality Partnership Report no. 20*. Australian Council of Social Service and UNSW Sydney. Retrieved from: https://povertyandinequality.acoss.org.au/wp-content/uploads/2023/03/Poverty-in-Australia-2023_Who-is-affected_screen.pdf

Davidson, P., Saunders, P., Bradbury, B. & Wong, M. (2020). *Poverty in Australia 2020: Part 1, Overview*. ACOSS/UNSW Poverty and Inequality Partnership Report No. 3, Sydney: ACOSS.

Deloitte Access Economics. (2018). Analysis of the impact of raising benefit rates. Australian Council of Social Service. Available from www.acoss.org.au/wp-content/uploads/2018/09/DAE-Analysis-of-the-impact-of-raising-benefit-rates-FINAL-4-September-...-1.pdf

Department of Employment and Workplace relations (DEWR). (2018). Job Seeker Compliance Public Data – June Quarter 2018. Retrieved from: www.dewr.gov.au/employment-research-and-statistics/resources/job-seeker-compliance-public-data-june-quarter-2018 (May 2023).

Department of Social Services (DSS). (2022). DSS Demographics – June 2022. Australian Government. Retrieved from: https://data.gov.au/data/dataset/cff2ae8a-55e4-47db-a66d-e177fe0ac6a0/resource/1188c950-542a-4ca6-9e3e-9f91f53d9314/download/dss-demographics-june-2022-final.xlsx

Ehrenreich, B. (2006). Barbara Ehrenreich on Poverty, War and Feminism's Place in the World on *DemocracyNow.Org Daily Show* – 27th of December [TV series]. DemocracyNow. Available from: www.democracynow.org/2006/12/27/barbara_ehrenreich_on_poverty_war_and

Galloway, A. (2023). *Voters favour tax breaks, childcare subsidies for working women over JobSeeker raise. Sydney Morning Herald*. Retrieved from: www.smh.com.au/politics/federal/voters-favour-tax-breaks-childcare-subsidies-for-working-women-over-jobseeker-raise-20230419-p5d1li.html

Gibson, M., Hearty, W., & Craig, P. (2018). *Universal basic income: A scoping review of evidence on impacts and study characteristics*. What Works Scotland.

Guerin, B. (2003). Putting a radical socialness into consumer behavior analysis. *Journal of Economic Psychology, 24*(5), 697–718. https://doi.org/10.1016/S0167-4870(03)00009-6

Guerin, B. (2016). *How to rethink human behavior: A practical guide to social contextual analysis*. Routledge.

Guerin, B. (2020). *Turning Psychology into a Social Science*. Routledge.

Guerin, B., Leugi, G. B., & Thain, A. (2018). Attempting to overcome problems shared by both qualitative and quantitative methodologies: Two hybrid procedures to encourage diverse research. *The Australian Community Psychologist, 29*(2), 74–90.

Haushofer, J., & Fehr, E. (2014). On the psychology of poverty. *Science, 344*(6186), 862–867. doi:10.1126/science.1232491

Henry, K., Harmer, J., Piggot, J., Ridout, H., & Smith, G. (2010). *Australia's future tax system (Part 1 and 2)*. Commonwealth Copyright Administration, Attorney-General's Department. Retrieved from: https://treasury.gov.au/review/the-australias-future-tax-system-review/final-report

Jacob, B., Pilkauskas, N., Rhodes, E., Richard, K., & Shaefer, H. L. (2022). The COVID-19 Cash Transfer Study II: The hardship and mental health impacts of an unconditional cash transfer to low-income individuals. *National Tax Journal, 75*(3), 597–627. https://link.gale.com/apps/doc/A723004998/AONE?u=unisa&sid=bookmark-AONE&xid=bc19f70c

Johnson, M. T., & Johnson, E. A. (2019). Stress, domination and basic income: Considering a citizens' entitlement response to a public health crisis. *Social Theory & Health, 17*, 253–271. http://dx.doi.org/10.1057/s41285-018-0076-3

Johnson, M. T., Johnson, E. A., Webber, L., & Nettle, D. (2020). Mitigating social and economic sources of trauma: The need for universal basic income during the coronavirus pandemic. *Psychological Trauma: Theory, Research, Practice, and Policy, 12*(S1), S191–S192. https://doi.org/10.1037/tra0000739

Kahneman, D. (2003). Maps of bounded rationality: Psychology for behavioral economics. *American Economic Review, 93*(5), 1449–1475. doi:10.1257/000282803322655392

Kangas, O., Jauhiainen, S., Simanainen, M., & Ylikännö, M. (2019). *The basic income experiment 2017–2018 in Finland: Preliminary results*. Ministry of Social Affairs. https://julkaisut.valtioneuvosto.fi/bitstream/handle/10024/161361/Report_TheBasicIncomeExperiment20172018inFinland.pdf?sequence=1&isAllowed=y

Kumar, S. L., Calvo-Friedman, A., Freeman, A. L., Fazio, D., Johnson, A. K., Seiferth, F., … & Doran, K. M. (2023). An unconditional cash transfer program for low-income New Yorkers affected by COVID-19. *Journal of Urban Health: Bulletin of the New York Academy of Medicine, 100*(1), 16–28. https://doi.org/10.1007/s11524-022-00693-9

Lea, S. E., Tarpy, R. M., & Webley, P. M. (1987). *The individual in the economy: A textbook of economic psychology*. CUP Archive.

Murphy, K. (2017). Ten years on, voters say labor's $52bn stimulus saved Australia from recession. *The Guardian*. www.theguardian.com/business/2017/aug/04/ten-years-on-voters-say-labors-52bn-stimulus-saved-australia-from-recession

Orshansky, M. (1969). How poverty is measured. *Monthly Labor Review, 92*, 37.

Polanyi, K. (1944/2001). *The great transformation: The political and economic origins of our time*. Beacon Press.

Rachlin, H. (1980). Economics and behavioral psychology. In J. E. R. Staddon (Ed.), *Limits to action: The allocation of individual behavior* (pp. 205–236). Academic Press.
Saunders, P. R. (2004). *Australia's welfare habit and how to kick it*. Duffy & Snellgrove Centre for Independent Studies.
Simmel, G. (1907/1971). *'Exchange'* [translated extract from Philosophie des Geldes. Leipzig, Duncker & Humbolt]. In G. Simmel (ed.), *On individuality and social form* (pp. 43–69). University of Chicago Press.
Simon, H. A. (1972). Theories of bounded rationality. In C. B. McGuire & R. Radner (eds.), *Decision and organization* (pp. 161–176). North Holland Publishing Company.
Summers, K. M., Deska, J. C., Almaraz, S. M., Hugenberg, K., & Lloyd, E. P. (2021). Poverty and pain: Low-SES people are believed to be insensitive to pain. *Journal of Experimental Social Psychology, 95,* Article 104116. https://doi.org/10.1016/j.jesp.2021.104116
Sunstein, C. R. (2017). Introduction "don't tell me what I can't do!": On the intrinsic value of control. In A. Samson (ed.), *The behavioural economics guide 2017*. Retrieved from www.behavioraleconomics.com
Wilson, N., & McDaid, S. (2021). The mental health effects of a Universal Basic Income: A synthesis of the evidence from previous pilots. *Social Science & Medicine, 287,* 114374–114374. https://doi.org/10.1016/j.socscimed.2021.114374
Wolf, M. (2018). Ain't misbehaving: Behavioral economics and the making of financial literacy. *Economic Sociology – The European Electronic Newsletter, 19*(2), 10–18.
Zafirovski, M. (2005). Social exchange theory under scrutiny: A positive critique of its economic-behaviorist formulations. *Electronic Journal of Sociology, 2*(2), 1–40.

2

WHAT IS POVERTY?

Before we can do anything about poverty, we have to know what it is. Let us start with the basics:

> Poverty: "*The state of one who lacks a usual or socially acceptable amount of money or material possessions.*"
>
> *(Merriam-Webster Dictionary, 2020)*

Poverty is not enough money or material possessions. Most people will reduce this to "not enough money". These answers make intuitive sense, but we know more is happening. What do we want money for? To buy the things we need or want (resources). Why do we want resources? They keep our lives going and, most importantly, our relationships working. Why do we want those relationships? To gain or maintain the opportunities, resources, and relationships they can provide for growth and new experience. This last link includes work/employment, which pays us money (Figure 2.1).

As children, we have this cycle short-circuited by our parents providing the resources directly but in modern life this cycle is still there, in the background. As we age, the variety of resources we get through money expands and can encompass everything from having food and a home to hobbies and entertainment or a social and political life. All of this happens in context, as what gives rise to our social behaviour:

> Men make their own history, but they do not make it as they please; they do not make it under self-selected circumstances, but under circumstances existing already, given, and transmitted from the past.
>
> *(Marx, 1852)*[1]

DOI: 10.4324/9781003453970-2

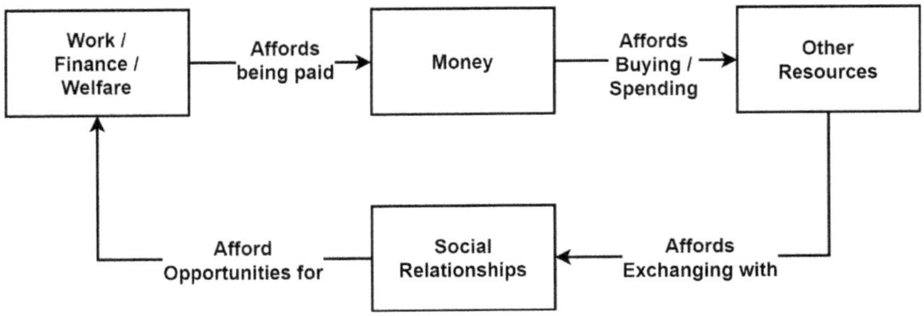

FIGURE 2.1 The basic process of our lives with money.

Poverty could be not having enough money. It could also be any other part of the cycle or something lacking in the wider context. To focus on money ignores the importance of people with whom exchanges of resources can occur (Guerin, 2016; Simmel, 1907/1971) and the meanings these exchanges provide (Daly, 2017; Zelizer, 1995). Choosing 'what poverty is' any one of these parts or processes is rather arbitrary, but this is not a new insight:

> For deciding who is poor, prayers are more relevant than calculation because poverty, like beauty, lies in the eye of the beholder.
>
> *(Orshansky, 1969, p. 37)*

Orshansky is the originator of the basket measure of poverty still used today in the United States. She used food and land data to develop a measure of the basic stable foods a family would need and the cost of that basket as a marker of poverty. Nevertheless, her insights are relevant today while we argue about what counts as poor and what we use to identify people experiencing poverty.

The definitions and concepts of poverty have expanded and splintered over time. Definitions range from simple ideas, like dictionary definitions, to complex academic conceptualisations, including money, or the absence of social relationships or 'having a voice in society' (Kanbur & Squire, 1999; Raphael, 2013). Most definitions still exist in some form (see Misturelli & Heffernan, 2012). We can use terms like 'not enough', 'socially acceptable amount', and 'decent' or 'social disadvantage' to place some boundaries around our discussion. Inevitably the abstraction seems to be simplified when it is measured as not enough money. We revert to money amounts because we have lots of readily available financial data, and comparisons and cut-offs are easily understood in dollar amounts (Coser, 1965, p. 143). Despite that simplification, you need a few complicating ideas to understand poverty better.

Absolute versus Relative

How do we determine enough? Where do we draw the line?
Do we set it at the minimum anyone needs or what you specifically need?
The minimum to live or the minimum to live well, happily and flourish?

These questions are the argument between absolute and relative definitions of poverty. Absolute poverty is when your resources are not enough for the 'most basic human needs'. Absolute poverty indicators include:

- Food/starvation
- Water/thirst
- Shelter/homelessness
- Basic/no education
- Access to information/no access
- Social services/social exclusion

People who experience absolute poverty most likely experience severe illness, and death is only narrowly avoided (Berleman, 1970, p. 27). Despite absolute poverty's concrete resources and relational elements, money is still the main measure. The World Bank's Dollar a Day is one absolute poverty line, though not so absolute as it was updated in 2015 to US$ 1.90. The measure is a proxy for those basic resources for living. The Dollar a Day absolute poverty line is applied only to the world's poorest people/places. Absolute poverty is a reality for ~767 million people worldwide as of 2013 (World Bank, 2016, p. 35).

Considering who is affected by absolute poverty brings us to the first major issue for discussing poverty, as someone presenting poverty in a Western, Colonised, Neoliberal, Capitalist, Developed, Industrial 'Northern' Economy of Australia. Most conceptions of poverty, particularly absolute poverty, are rare or non-existent in industrialised economies (McDonald, 2013). Wagle (2017, p. 10) says it is "ludicrous" to apply absolute measures to countries like Australia. That said, the most disadvantaged of Australia, often with overrepresentation of Aboriginal and Torres Strait Islander Peoples, often go without basic needs even if they technically have more money than the proxy thresholds due to disruptions in their contexts through colonisation (Saunders, 1996 in Australian Bureau of Statistics, 1301.0). This issue will appear again – concepts are designed for populations unlike Australian peoples and economics – none the less I want to discuss these ideas for how they may help you understand real experiences.

Our other option is to set the line based on the needs or the expected minimums of the countries and people rather than the absolutes needed for human life. Relative poverty is a set of things needed to successfully participate as part of a given society, an amount of something considered 'decent' that changes depending on context. Relative poverty has always been present. For example, Adam Smith's Wealth of Nations (1776/2007, p. 676) includes, "By necessaries I understand not only the commodities which are indispensably necessary for the support of life, but whatever the custom of the country renders it indecent for creditable people, even of the lowest order, to be without". Necessaries could include anything important or needed to live well in any particular place and time. For Smith it was leather shoes and a linen shirt. Furthermore, needs change based on who you are – someone with a disability or major health condition may need different things compared to someone otherwise able-bodied.

Unfortunately, despite the freer form relative poverty allows, it is still largely measured in monetary terms. For economies like Australia and the UK, this is usually measured as 50% or 60% of a country'*s median income*, or a standardised 'basket of goods' (see Deeming, 2005, 2017; Orshansky, 1969; Saunders & Bedford, 2017).

The issue with defaulting to money again is that even if you have enough money, you may have other things interrupting you from getting those needed resources. Such issues have been known for over 100 years and throughout most poverty research. In Rowntree's (1901/1908, p. 87) landmark study of poverty, he noted that drinking, betting, and gambling, as well as "improvident expenditure induced by irregularity of income" (p. 142), interrupted the income for those needed resources. Rowntree stressed that these behaviours were likely caused by poor living conditions and not the other way around (pp. 144–145). The point to take away is *that having 'enough' income, absolute or relative, does not describe all the context for obtaining the resources you need.*

Multidimensionality

Which one is it, then?
Not money, food, shelter, a job, or a social life?
Do we need to consider everything?

'Multidimensional' is a term you will read in poverty literature, referring to the many things we must consider. Treating poverty as multidimensional means we combine tangible and intangible indicators (e.g., food and sense of security). Most conceptions of poverty include some degree of multidimensionality.

The 2018 revision to the United Nations Development Programme (UNDP) Multidimensional Poverty Index (MPI) is a recent example of constructing poverty as multidimensional (Alkire & Jahan, 2018). The UNDP Global MPI uses conceptual dimensions, including health, education, and living standards. The concrete *indicators* include nutrition, child mortality, years of school attendance, cooking fuel, sanitation, drinking water, electricity, housing, and assets.

Again, in Australia, poverty by these indicators is likely rare. The Human Development Index is a counterpart to the MPI, which measures life expectancy, years of education, and gross national income. This multidimensional index shows that in 2018 Australia placed third, behind Norway and Switzerland, with a 0.939 score (UNDP, 2018). However, the MPI can be adjustable to the "much different" forms of deprivation found in nations (White, 2017, p. 2). Multidimensional indicators are also constructed specifically for Australia (e.g., Scutella et al., 2013). We also obviously cannot claim there is no poverty in Australia, so we will need to consider multidimensionality even if established tools are unusable.

Multidimensionality even appears when asking directly about money. I asked one of my participants Emily, a young single mother, "What do you think your control of money is like? Do you think you are good at controlling money?" initially, she said "No!" but continued to say:

> I don't want to be so tightly wrapped and controlled in my life; I just want to go out and spend heaps of money and have a good time. I just don't want to feel that. Of course, I think money controls me largely, I'd say it limits what I can and can't do. My ability to earn is controlled because of my situation.

She then explained that she buys things impulsively but questioned what I meant by the word 'control'. Then she gave this heartfelt response, being wrapped and controlled by money which is the heart of what I want to tell you about in this book. Complex contexts make this answer real for Emily; she experiences precarious employment, difficult postgraduate study, and the everyday struggles of being a poor single mother. Emily speaks directly to the contextual pressures of living in poverty, the issues around how and when to spend money, momentarily impulsive but 'tightly wrapped' in what is ultimately possible – even earning more money.

Types of Poverty and Satellite Concepts

There are many measures and conceptualisations of poverty, including income approaches, material deprivation, social exclusion, and the capabilities approach. A set of poverty concepts are in Table 2.1. The primary purpose here is to briefly highlight their *conceptual design*, not their mathematical measurement. The conceptualisation, and concrete indicators, can be asked about when you work directly with someone. I sought throughout my research to understand the everyday behaviours that people carry out to obtain the resources and experiences shown in Table 2.1.

TABLE 2.1 Types of Poverty Described with Example Measures

Type	*Description*
Income poverty	Measuring poverty by the amount of money someone has moving through their exchanges (cashflow, wages, salary, benefits, pensions, dividends, or inheritance) **Example (Australian):** 50% national median income 2017–2018 for a single person • AU$ 23,764 per year/AU$ 457 per week (before housing costs) (Davidson et al., 2020, p. 12)
Material deprivation	Measuring poverty by lacking a set number of items from a list defined as 'needed' because 'they could not be afforded'. **Example (Australia):** A consensual list of items from the HILDA survey including: • Getting together with friends or relatives for a drink or meal at least once a month • Medical treatment when needed • Furniture in reasonable condition • A decent and secure home • A week's holiday away from home each year • Access to the Internet at home • *Over a dozen other items in the full list* (see Saunders & Wilkins, 2016, p. 85)
Social exclusion	A collection of items and experiences that demonstrate social, cultural, and political participation. **Example (Australia)** Access to or ownership of many different indicators in these domains: • Material resources (largely housing and income) • Employment • Education and skills • Health and disability • Social (including internet access) • Community (e.g., transport and civic participation) • Personal safety (see Scutella et al., 2013)
Capability approach/ deprivation	A person's ability to utilise commodities for life flourishing, for example, transport is only possible with a bicycle if you can ride it; if not, the bicycle does not afford the transport capability. **Example (international abstract list applicable to Australia)** General life domains whose list of specific elements will change depending on the nation, place, time, community, and individual, including: • Life • Bodily health • Bodily integrity • Senses, imagination, and thought • Emotions • Practical reason • Affiliation • Other species • Play • Control over one's environment (political and material) (Central Capabilities by Nussbaum, 2003)

Now that you have seen the basic components of these major poverty and poverty-related concepts let us consider their implementation and implications for a country like Australia.

Income Poverty

Today, in countries like Australia, we 'get by' by working with strangers to get money and accumulate capital. Of most relevance here is benefits – largely unemployment and disability pensions. If the amount you earn via these methods is insufficient to sustain buying the norm, you have found the poor and observed poverty.

Currently, and surprisingly, the Australian government does not officially track or endorse a measure of poverty. The standard measure of relative income poverty in an affluent country like Australia is 50% of the median income before or after housing costs (see Table 2.1). Australia has another unofficial poverty line, the Henderson Poverty Line (HPL). The HPL is based on the $62.70 per week benchmark income from the 1975 Henderson Poverty Inquiry, updated quarterly and matched to Household Disposable Income per week per capita (in December 2017: AU$ 518.16 per week; Melbourne Institute, 2017).

The common 50% median income indicator is hotly contested. Some suggest a 60% median, to cover the many people struggling to make ends meet (Saunders & Bedford, 2017). Others suggest entirely different calculations of poverty (see other concepts below). The dispute arises because so much is left out in an income analysis. Families have different needs, so some families with income above these relative lines may still not participate fully in Australian society or go without elements considered necessary as judged by the population (relative) or even for health (absolute).

Furthermore, basic living standards are affected by many influences beyond income (see Saunders & Wong, 2008). Ultimately, income poverty is a narrow measure. It hides the concrete things you need, like food and shelter, and the everyday social life we really care about. Without more investigation, there is no way of knowing purely from income if those categorised as 'in poverty' are observably and recognisably 'poor' in a qualitative or descriptive sense – though it is highly likely.

Deprivation

Deprivation is useful to overcome the above issues of income poverty. Deprivation is when someone lacks something vital for life or participation in society. Deprivation does not replace income poverty but is more like verification; to see if the income poverty line reflects the material experience of the poor. In many ways, measuring deprivation by material goods to validate income poverty is a step backwards. Some of the original poverty lines were calculated by costing needed material goods and services, such as Rowntree's (1901/1908) study, which based monetary poverty lines on what the citizens of York needed to buy to live successfully, or Orshansky's Poverty Thresholds (1963, 1965) based on a nutritionally adequate diet. Still today, many new poverty lines are suggested or evaluated by food basket-based minimums and show the mismatch between arbitrary income lines and real experiences (see Saunders & Bedford, 2017 for an Australian example). The focus of the concept of deprivation is not on income but on real access to things necessary for a good life.

The entangled and complex relationships between 'specific' deprivation and 'general' poverty cannot be understated. Adam Smith (1776/2007) noted the need to participate in society without shame, notably needing a clean linen shirt and leather shoes – without which you might not earn an income. Such appeals to shame as core to the poverty experience have been found across national and economic borders (see Walker et al., 2013).

Relative deprivation can also be traced back to social psychological investigations (Stouffer et al., 1949). This research focuses on the comparisons people make between themselves and those immediately around them in context. Runciman (1966) used a formal system regarding an object X by person A:

Person A does not have X
Person A knows of other persons that have X
Person A wants to have X
Person A believes obtaining X is realistic

Runciman also put forward categories of relative deprivation: *egoistic* individual comparisons where the comparisons are in-group and *fraternal* group-level comparisons to other 'better off' groups. Merton (1968) expanded the idea with reference group theory and formal applications. Alongside relative deprivation and comparison work in social psychology and sociology, relative deprivation has focused on the intergroup and intragroup relationships via the perceived unjust distribution of resources (for a review, see Pettigrew, 2015). In poverty research deprivation's conception is rather separate from this psychological mechanism; however, there is a reliance on the psychological process allowing people to be verbally or cognitively aware of their deprivation compared to others.

Poverty researchers, when talking about deprivation, mostly refer to the work of Peter Townsend (1979). Townsend produced an analysis of how deprivation was affecting British families. There was a separation between the material conditions of deprivation as he investigated and the psychological "feelings" (see pp. 47–48). Townsend summarised poverty by relative deprivation as:

> Individuals, families and groups in the population can be said to be in poverty when they lack the resources to obtain the types of diet, participate in the activities and have the living conditions and amenities which are customary or are at least widely encouraged or approved, in the societies to which they belong. Their resources are so seriously below those commanded by the average individual or family that they are, in effect, excluded from ordinary living patterns, customs and activities.
>
> *(Townsend, 1979, p. 31)*

Townsend developed a list of objects and experiences for measuring deprivation, separate from people's feelings about their deprivation (see pp. 413–431). Some deprivation indicators were food, clothing, fuel (for heat), housing or shelter, amenities, safety, family support, recreational activities, education, general and mental health, social relationships, and community participation (Townsend, 1979, p. 249). Townsend's deprivation index asks about more direct experiences, for example, "Adults only. Has not had a relative or friend to the home for a meal or snack in the last four weeks" as an example of social participation (Townsend, 1979, p. 250). Many social researchers since Townsend, notably Mack and Lansley (1985), have suggested many general and population-specific sets of 'needed goods' to determine deprivation. By asking the public what they think is necessary, simple things like public transport and a warm coat were high on the list of needs.

When Townsend compared the feelings (psychology) of deprivation to the objective index, something interesting arose. The findings contain the curious case that many who were poor, as measured by the contemporary British state standard, and deprived, as measured by Townsend, denied being in poverty. Reasons for denial included *stability of personal circumstances, frequent social contacts, or other feelings of deprivation*. While these people did not admit they were poor, they accepted they had difficulties managing incomes compared to others (p. 426).

Similarly, nearly a third of all respondents denied the existence of poverty in Britain. Reasons for this denial included: *generalising their attitudes towards people experiencing poverty or select groups of the poor*, such as thinking poor people were the irresponsible unemployed; *pessimistic or fatalistic attitudes towards helping those less fortunate*, that it is just bad luck; *opinions directed to stop helping people experiencing poverty* as well as *optimistic attitudes* implying people need to help themselves or will otherwise get the help they need (pp. 427–428). What is interesting in this denial of poverty is that in a wealthy country, we can imagine that more people are deprived even if they are not income-poor, given so many resources are needed to participate successfully in that society (Townsend, 1979, p. 31) but also because this data suggests many people are deprived even if they do not report they are.

Specific Australian applications of deprivation now exist, for example, the Household, Income and Labour Dynamics in Australia (HILDA) survey material deprivation measure. Participants are asked to judge a list of resources as necessary or not for Australian life. Then asks whether participants had those resources, and if they did not, whether this was due to an inability to afford them. The indicated necessary resources from the HILDA survey appear in Table 2.1. Saunders and Wilkins (2016, HILDA wave 14) found that in 2014 11.6% of Australians were deprived of two or more key indicators, and 6.6% of three or more.

Social Exclusion

'Participation' as a threshold reoccurs throughout poverty literature. Having resources means nothing if you cannot do something with them. Social exclusion/inclusion is what I call a 'satellite' concept of poverty. Poverty conceptualisation has affected this concept and vice versa but they are not synonymous.

Social exclusion is a phrase traced back to Rene Lenoir (1974) in *Les Exclus: Un Francais sur dix* which said that for many reasons, including age, mental illness, disability, trauma, or single-parent status, citizens of France were becoming excluded from welfare systems which provided support based on employment but such groups of people often could not or were not allowed to work they were excluded from citizens common rights. The things that people participate in which the poor are excluded from often include many of the common 'poverty indicators', for example, Silver (1994): employment, housing, education, various forms of capital, public goods, family, a social life, and abstract elements such as fulfilment and understanding.

Exclusion is more about what you do than what you have. What do people need to be part of a community or society – friendship, fulfilment, a sense of belonging?

> [Poverty is the] lack of material resources, especially income, necessary to participate in British society ... [social exclusion] refers to the dynamic process of being shut out, fully or partially, from any of the social, economic, political and cultural systems which determine the social integration of a person in society.
>
> *(Walker & Walker, 1997, p. 8)*

Social exclusion, therefore, while separate from poverty, is key to the discussion. Someone excluded has limited chances to gain income or material goods. Similarly, someone deprived or on a low income will be excluded due to limited resources excluding them from everyday social life. As in Figure 2.1, the cycle of getting by is broken just as much by money as it is by resources as it is by relationships: for example, a homeless person is not able to get a job from someone else because they do not have the money to buy clean appropriate clothing for an interview. Note that with these social processes meaningfully in our thinking, we can better address health, mental well-being, political activity, and freedom issues arising from poverty.

Unfortunately, academic literature and policy over the last several decades have measured exclusion, deprivation, and poverty similarly. An example of social exclusion in Australia is Scutella et al.'s (2013) analysis. They included seven domains with multiple components each (see Table 2.1). You should be able to notice the overlap between the lists throughout the concepts. The overlap may be because HILDA survey data is used to generate 29 indicators which are also true for our Australian deprivation indicators. Other applications like the Social Exclusion Monitor by the Brotherhood of St Laurence and the Melbourne Institute (2020) gave weights to over 30 indicators of the 2018 HILDA data, resulting in 25% of Australians measured as excluded (19% marginally and 6% deeply) consistent since 2009. While they rightly claim that social exclusion is a better measure than income poverty, unfortunately, we have no information on real social relationships because the data is a survey of individual self-reports, simply of whether the respondent experiences an indicator. While important conceptually, exclusion becomes difficult to separate from deprivation when indicators used are so starkly alike, or in this case, the same.

Still, the concept of social exclusion re-introduces social relationships to the processes of poverty: not just, 'Are the poor hungry?' but questions such as 'with whom can they eat?'; and not just, 'Are the poor employed?', but 'who can get them a job?'. Potentially, focusing more on the exclusion elements may yield important revelations, for example, 'Who refuses to eat with them?' or 'Who refuses them a job and why?'.

Capabilities Approach

There is, however, an aspect of many of the above elements of poverty, deprivation, and exclusion that are left unanalysed: for what do we need these resources or this participation? That question leads us to another satellite concept; Amartya Sen's highly popular *capabilities approach* (Sen, 1980, 1984, 1999) is highly praised for its insights into global development and poverty. The capabilities approach is unique in its people-focused economic development instead of the financial-focus. The approach is primarily concerned with 'substantive freedoms', the ability to choose and do things in everyday life for oneself. Sen argues that measuring commodities is not enough to understand development and freedom. For the capabilities approach, commodities are useful due to the functionings the commodity allows. Depending upon their history and context, everyone can exercise some of these functionings, which gives the commodity value. When someone has a commodity and a capability, they can exercise it to do and be what they want, which means living a freer life than if that capability were deprived. Poverty, then, will be a function of material deprivation *and* individual capabilities. Some definitions of poverty have been derived from Sen's work (e.g., Van den Bosch, 2001).

An example given by Sen (1999, p. 6) is that ownership of a bicycle as a commodity is not the same as being able (capable) to use the bicycle functionally (to go cycling); for example, someone physically disabled might be unable to ride a bicycle even if they own one. The initial approach by Sen was *absolute yet* gave no set list of capabilities. Sen acknowledged that the commodities needed for freedom would be relative. The capabilities approach has since been developed to include lists of capabilities. One such theoretically defined list is the *Central Capabilities* from Nussbaum (2003, 2011; Table 2.1). Nussbaum argued for a definite list, but that it would still change with context. Nussbaum's list is general, which means it was made – again – for countries that are not as capitalistically industrialised as Australia, yet the list is still applicable in this context.

Popularity, however, does not mean that the concept is without its criticisms and shortcomings. Primarily, the individualistic assumptions, focused on choice, found within the theory have drawn criticism (Dean, 2009, pp. 266–267; Robeyns, 2005, pp. 107–109). Individuals have their capabilities, which can lead to isolating the problem of capability deprivation inside the person as an issue about how they choose, potentially increasing the concepts' ability to blame the deprived for their situation. Also problematic is that external influences, such as government-provided welfare, could interfere with personal freedom to choose, depriving capabilities. Benefits and other government programmes to promote behaviour may be seen as reducing freedom. It is dangerous to presuppose that the issue is a person's choices; rather, we need to know the resources, relationships, and contexts for their behaviours and check the assumption that people experiencing poverty have a choice or power to decide what to do with their economics.

Beyond that problem, the issue of relativity has sparked a debate. The capabilities approach is rarely applied to the economically 'developed' or 'Economically Northern' nations, as Sen considers it an absolute concept. Townsend and Sen have debated if relative or absolute capabilities from commodities were appropriate (Sen, 1983, 1985; Townsend, 1985, 1993, pp. 130–137; also see Lister, 2004). Townsend argued that the relative nature of what is needed in a context means, therefore, capabilities change with context. Sen agreed there is relativity for the commodities needed but argued that capabilities themselves, whatever they are, are absolute – Sen seemingly appealing to moral positions on who is the worst off, such as those starving or hungry. Townsend argued that such moral judgements on who is worse off make the application ambiguous and not absolute, given that many people who are starving in 'developed' economies, such as the UK and Australia, can choose where to spend their income, so they may not be considered capability deprived even if they were starving (Sen, 1983, p. 159; Townsend, 1985, pp. 663–664). You will note that these points echo the worries about individualism and choice mentioned above. Hence, the application of capabilities requires care to avoid blaming.

Robeyns (2005), followed by Deneulin (2011), argued that capabilities are a framework for understanding social issues, but other new theories are needed to explain poverty, exclusion, and deprivation. Deneulin (2011) further said there are many approaches in the 'capability tradition', such as 'liberal-evaluative' and 'relational-political' interpretations. Liberal interpretations focus on individuals' freedom and good life, regardless of oppression; this is an 'ethical individualist' position, considering individuals' feelings on their choices and context. The relational interpretation states that individuals cannot be separated from their context and relationships in the 'structures of living together'. The relational structures are assessed for how value and a common 'good life' come from systems influencing individuals related to one another, for good or ill. For the application later in this book, we look at individual cases (people) *with others in context* (see Figure 2.1) and therefore align with the relational interpretation of capabilities.

Subjective Poverty

In the discussion of Townsend's deprivation, we discussed the feeling of poor people saying they were not poor while the measures suggested they were. Subjective poverty privileges those 'subjective feelings' over others' 'objective' examination. Subjective poverty, in practice, is the ability within studies of *the reported personal experience of the individual to determine whether they are in poverty* without some defining element outside of this self-determination (money, material goods, or acts of social exclusion). Similarly, *consensual poverty analysis* sets lines of income poverty, material deprivation indicators, or exclusion experiences by asking for the view of the population and coming to some common indicators and thresholds (see Van den Bosch, 2001).

Saunders et al. (1994) suggest that when defining poverty,

> it is now widely accepted that poverty is a normative rather than purely objective concept ... issues of value and ideology inevitably arise in the selection of a standard ... any definition of poverty must be made in a

> specific social (and moral) context and only has meaning relative to that context.
>
> *(p. 6)*

The 1994 study asks the opinion of its participants, Australian and Swedish, what amount they believe is enough "to make ends meet". Swedish and Australian samples suggested about US$ 300 a week (US$ 600 today) – with 21% of Australia in poverty by this measure. More recent examples of consensual lines include Saunders and Bedford's (2017) budget standard for Australia and the questions in the HILDA survey on material deprivation.

Social–Relational Poverty

Now we move to some complicating factors for the five above concepts. While people experiencing poverty are often considered separate from society, especially through concepts like social exclusion, the poor still rely on exchanges with others to get by. We often ask or count the things they have or do not have, but that hides the processes and behaviours of getting and having. More worrying is that relationships are *absent* in theories on poverty. Social–relational investigations, like exclusion, focus on how people behave together to become poor or non-poor. Social exclusion often analyses how cultural patterns, identities, or discriminatory behaviour stop people from interacting with one another (Madanipour et al., 2015; Silver, 1994). We need concepts and methods which include both resources and social relationships:

> The definition of what it is to be poor is something which comes out of the relations between people.
>
> *(Halsey, 1985, p. 45)*

Social–relational approaches examine people interacting and how they effect poverty. Relational poverty research is more prominent in anthropology (see Desmond, 2014, for a review), sociology (Zelizer, 2010), health studies (Hodgetts & Stolte, 2017), and geographical studies (Mosse, 2010; Shelton, 2018). These all argue poverty cannot be separated from the wealth and freedom experienced by the affluent. The social relationships, between the middle class, the rich, and the poor, through their economic exchanges, simultaneously generate both the expenses the poor struggle to keep up with and are the additional sources of income the affluent benefit from. We cannot forget that poor people are poor, often for the same reasons rich people are rich.

An important expansion of the idea of relational poverty analysis comes from geography (Lawson, 2012). This relational analysis shows the material and discursive struggles as the middle class are confronted with people experiencing poverty. The intersections of age, gender, caste, and class (Lawson, 2012, p. 8) are like those found in social exclusion because how people talk and act with others is how poverty happens. Those everyday behaviours around material deprivation or labelling and understanding people as poor are the process by which the exclusion of people experiencing poverty occurs – someone not wanting to employ a person on benefits, for example – but this happens while maintaining the exchanges between both groups – that unemployed person still pays rent to those with capital (Shelton, 2018). More research is still needed on the contexts of the non-poor, or 'affluent', as they relate to poverty and poor people, and how both the poor and non-poor act against or with each other in the political economy, governance, and cultural politics.

A direct example of the system benefiting the rich and making the poor poorer is a well-known aspect of the Australian housing market. For example, during this investigation, housing availability to those low-income Australian found that out of 67,000 properties reviewed, only 3 (0.05%) were affordable to a single person on NewStart (Anglicare Australia, 2018). Australians on these payments are still paying rent for properties giving an alarming proportion of their income to property owners, helping maintain those owners as affluent. In 2015–2016, 51% of low-income earners were in housing stress (over 30% of their income going to housing costs; ABS, 4130.0, 2017). Acknowledging relational poverty seems slow, but available data supports a focus on who benefits from poverty. However, these arguments are not isolated to Australia (see Shelton, 2018). Also notable is that the above trends have become significantly worse for everyone after COVID-19.

Relational types of investigation, such as those above, have started to reformulate poverty, deprivation, and exclusion more directly as *behaviour through social relationships* rather than a setlist of objects or behaviours an individual does or has alone.

The Time Scale of Poverty

Throughout the literature, both discussion of the concepts and critiques, there was a distinct lack of discussion about the length of time people are poor, deprived, or excluded. Some studies did check things over time, but this was usually just asking about a variable again later (e.g., Headey, 2006, p. 6), not an examination of what it is like to stay in poverty for a long time or what it is like to move in and out of poverty:

> [Community Social Psychology is] compatible with the concept of poverty as a socially constructed process. Poverty is temporary and changeable. This contrasts with a hegemonic understanding of poverty, which universalises and/or fragments, and in which the poor have no role to play.
>
> *(Sánchez et al., 2003, p. 138)*

Hulme and Shepard (2003) offer a unique perspective as they critically consider and critique the common one-off population measure of poverty. Starting with a critique of the Dollar a Day poverty line, they develop an attack on the idea of people experiencing poverty as a homogeneous group, and more directly that most policies in the developing world were aimed at reducing poverty of the income poor and the "deserving" and "easy to assist poor" (p. 404). They suggest that 'developed' nations usually have transient poverty in contrast to 'developing' nations of having mostly chronic poverty.

The chronic poor are those who are poor "for much of their life course" (p. 405) and may pass it on generationally. However, chronic poverty is given as a five-year window of poverty for measuring. Hulme and Shepard give a five-tier category system ranging from *always poor* through *usually poor, churning poor, occasionally poor,* and, finally, *never poor*. Using Bangladeshi data, their analysis found ten-year changes between their categories, from *never poor* to *always poor*, and all other categories except *always poor* to *never poor*, or *usually poor* to *never poor*. The data of Hulme and Shepard and their general conception imply that time is not just a factor in measuring poverty but is deeply intertwined with its experience. Again, Hulme and Shepard's concept is given for global development purposes, but that does not exclude these ideas from a broader application like in Australia. Particularly, we expect to find many *churning* and *occasionally* poor Australians who constantly move over and under poverty indicators.

How time presents itself in the social–psychological experience of poverty is essential as a general concept. How do people talk about their past or future in or out of poverty? Whom can they talk to about these things? What are the consequences of previous experiences of economic downturns on the choices made? How do the poor view their future? Psychology, at the least, should investigate the anxiety for the future of poverty and its effects on material goods, income, and relationships.

What Have We Learned?

Each of the concepts above adds something unique to the notion of what poverty is. Many unique ideas exist between these concepts, and the initial definition of not enough. Consider these differences when considering the solutions to, psychology of, and cases of poverty I will discuss. Each lens will let you see something different. I am not advocating that all measures be implemented together but rather anyone considering poverty should not do so narrowly. My case analyses in later chapters considered all my learning presented above while never privileging it over the experience of my participants. Table 2.2 displays how the many concepts of this chapter come together.

The rest of this book will consider these concepts for *qualities* in context. Focusing on qualities, processes, and relations diverges from the *quantity* focus

TABLE 2.2 Concepts of Poverty with a Comparison of Concept Qualities

Concepts	*Common measurement*	*Relative or absolute*	*Social–relational*	*Timescale*
Income	Dollar income	Both	No	Rarely (repeats)
Deprivation	Setlist of items, often material items	Relative	Deprivers implied	Rarely (repeats)
Exclusion	Setlist of qualities experienced or not	Relative	Behaviour with others, Excluders implied	Prolonged but not explicit
Capabilities	A stable list of Central Capabilities – ambiguousobservability	Relative commodities, Absolute capabilities	Contextually bound but individualist	Rarely (repeats)
Subjective poverty	Consensual poverty lines (income), Item-based methods, Personal identification	Relative	Dependent on application	Dependent on application

of 'counting the poor', often done by income and material measures due to the high availability of data (Coser, 1965, p. 143). So, consider the elements of Table 2.1, and realise this is all poverty and should all be considered when trying to understand the experience.

A final issue arises with assumptions in research and measurement. Most investigations are based on representative samples that list what resources and experiences in each society are necessary. Two assumptions complicate such tasks. First, it is assumed participants know the necessary items for the potentially undisclosed and challenging to define purpose: 'successful participation in society'. Second, it is assumed that participants can accurately report such a list without considering who is asking, when they ask, how they ask, or why they are asking. A functional view of language shows the remarkable effect of assumptions on data, especially when simple questions and answers with strangers are treated as neutral or usual answers (Guerin et al., 2018). Do you tell strangers what you really think and feel?

Sociological insights tell us that social changes through primarily cultural and religious contexts played, and still play, significant and changing roles in the economic development of everyday behaviour and the multiple and different views of 'enough' (Polanyi, 1944/2001; Weber, 1947/1964). For example, this book's primary data collection does not capture the unique needs that arose from the COVID-19 pandemic. Such insights tell us that agreed lists are about when and who was asked and are rarely static over context.

The issue of flux in needs is compounded by the fact that people may learn what is commonly necessary by interacting with media about what experts say is necessary, a phenomenon sometimes known as 'the double hermeneutic' (Giddens, 1986, pp. 284–285, 1987, p. 20). For example, agreeing on the need for dental check-ups may be influenced by doctors, dentists, public health researchers, and policy advisors who affect public knowledge by consistently advertising and suggesting that these check-ups are required to live well. The public may then agree to dental check-ups being on the list as necessary while, in their everyday life, avoiding dental check-ups with no worry. Further, other needed things may not appear on these lists should we not often speak about those needs (e.g., sexual needs are rare in the above concepts). Some may argue that allowing anonymity counters such reporting biases, but anonymity introduces the counterproductive possibility of increased lying (Lelkes et al., 2012). Instead, awareness of these issues, and the social nature of research, suggests that observations over time are needed to understand how people feel about labelling something as 'needed'.

When we all agree on 'what poverty is', we should recognise that this is just agreeing to say similar things compared to the people around us. So, when asking people what is needed, they tell us what they often hear people say is needed; such issues of verbal responses have been raised many times in the past (e.g., Mills, 1940; Guerin et al., 2018, p. 77; Nisbet & Wilson, 1977; Potter & Edwards, 1990). We may record stories rather than experiences.

So, not only will I discuss poverty in the following chapters as a complex and multi-faceted phenomenon, exploring the money, resources, and relationships in context, but I will also consider how people talk about themselves and poverty in general as a much more socially bound behaviour than you may expect. Considering both the world and discursive practice, to me, is how we remain critical and open to the issues remaining for understanding poverty.

Conclusion

I have tried to distil everything I read to answer the question 'what is poverty?' but really, I have no one answer. Many ideas are right and that complicates poverty research. Nevertheless, the solution going forward can be to understand poverty from people who self-identify and are observed as poor using these many concepts. Such research also needs to find a way to present data from such multidimensional explorations, as others are attempting (Hodgetts et al., 2019). While this chapter suggests limited usefulness in counting the poor or indicators of poverty, the point *remains that we should think about all these elements if we want to understand and do something about poverty, potentially even rethinking "the poor" as not a single group that policies effect evenly and equally.*

Note

1 My obligatory Marx reference, keep an eye out for the obligatory Orwell reference.

References

Alkire, S. and Jahan, S. (2018). The New Global MPI 2018: Aligning with the Sustainable Development Goals, *HDRO Occasional Paper,* United Nations Development Programme (UNDP).

Anglicare Australia. (2018). *Rental affordability snapshot 2018.* Anglicare Australia.

Australian Bureau of Statistics (ABS). (2017). *Housing Occupancy and Costs, 2015-16* (No. 4130.0). Retrieved from https://www.abs.gov.au/AUSSTATS/abs@.nsf/allprimarymainfeatures/3BD5C13D36DD892CCA2584390017BCCE?opendocument

Australian Bureau of Statistics (ABS). (1996). *Poverty and deprivation in Australia* (No. 1301.0). Retrieved from www.abs.gov.au/ausstats/abs@.nsf/0/5D709B83B7F7C25ECA2569DE00221C86

Berleman, W. C. (1970). Poverty—Some dilemmas in definition. *Growth and Change, 1*(4), 27–32. https://doi.org/10.1111/j.1468-2257.1970.tb00123.x

Brotherhood of St Laurence and the Melbourne Institute of Applied Economic and Social Research (MIAESR) (2020). *Social Exclusion Monitor*. Available: www.bsl.org.au/research/social-exclusion-monitor/

Coser, L. (1965). The sociology of poverty: To the memory of Georg Simmel. *Social Problems, 13*(2), 140–148. doi:10.2307/798899

Daly, M. (2017). Money-related meanings and practices in low-income and poor families. *Sociology, 51*(2), 450–465. https://doi.org/10.1177/0038038515616355

Davidson, P., Saunders, P., Bradbury, B., & Wong, M. (2020). *Poverty in Australia 2020: Part 1, Overview*. ACOSS/UNSW Poverty and Inequality Partnership Report No. 3. ACOSS.

Dean, H. (2009). Critiquing capabilities: The distractions of a beguiling concept. *Critical Social Policy, 29*(2), 261–278. doi:10.1177/0261018308101629

Deeming, C. (2005). Minimum income standards: How might budget standards be set for the UK? *Journal of Social Policy, 34*(4), 619–636. doi:10.1017/S0047279405009189

Deeming, C. (2017). Defining minimum income (and living) standards in Europe: Methodological issues and policy debates. *Social Policy and Society, 16*(1), 33–48. doi:10.1017/S147474641500041X

Deneulin, S. (2011, June). The Capability tradition: a note on two interpretations. In *a conference on human development at the University of Bielefeld, Germany* (Vol. 25, p. 26).

Desmond, M. (2014). Relational ethnography. *Theory and Society, 43*(5), 547–579. doi:10.1007/s11186-014-9232-5

Giddens, A. (1986). *The constitution of society: Outline of the theory of structuration*. Polity Press.

Giddens, A. (1987). *Social theory and modern sociology*. Stanford University Press.

Guerin, B. (2016). *How to rethink human behavior: A practical guide to social contextual analysis*. Routledge.

Guerin, B., Leugi, G. B., & Thain, A. (2018). Attempting to overcome problems shared by both qualitative and quantitative methodologies: Two hybrid procedures to encourage diverse research. *The Australian Community Psychologist, 29*(2), 74.

Headey, B. (2006). *A framework for assessing poverty, disadvantage and low capabilities in Australia*. Melbourne Institute of Applied Economic and Social Research.

Hodgetts, D., & Stolte, O. (2017). *Urban poverty and health inequalities: A relational approach*. Routledge.

Hodgetts, D., Stolte, O., King, P., & Groot, S. (2019). Reproducing the general through the local: Lessons from poverty research. In C. Højholt & E. Schraube (eds.), *Subjectivity and knowledge* (pp. 157–174). Springer. https://doi.org/10.1007/978-3-030-29977-4

Hulme, D., & Shepherd, A. (2003). Conceptualizing chronic poverty. *World Development, 31*(3), 403–423. doi:10.1016/S0305-750X(02)00222-X

Kanbur, L., & Squire, L. (1999). The evolution of thinking about poverty: Exploring the interaction. *Ninth Bradford Development Lecture, DPPC*. Bradford: University of Bradford.

Lawson, V. (2012). Decentring poverty studies: Middle class alliances and the social construction of poverty. *Singapore Journal of Tropical Geography, 33*(1), 1–19. doi:10.1111/j.1467-9493.2012.00443.x

Lelkes, Y., Krosnick, J. A., Marx, D. M., Judd, C. M., & Park, B. (2012). Complete anonymity compromises the accuracy of self-reports. *Journal of Experimental Social Psychology, 48*(6), 1291–1299.

Lenoir, R. (1974). *Les Exclus: Un Francais sur dix*. Seuil.

Lister, R. (2004). *Poverty*. Polity Press.

Mack, J., & Lansley, S. (1985). *Poor Britain*. George Allen & Unwin.

Madanipour, A., Shucksmith, M., & Talbot, H. (2015). Concepts of poverty and social exclusion in Europe. *Local Economy, 30*(7), 721–741. doi:10.1177/0269094215601634

Marx, K. (1852). *The Eighteenth Brumaire of Louis Bonaparte*. Progress Publishers.

McDonald, C. (2013). Poverty in Australia and the social work response. *Asia Pacific Journal of Social Work and Development, 23*(1), 3–11. https://doi.org/10.1080/02185385.2012.760233

Melbourne Institute of Applied Economic and Social Research. (2017). *Poverty lines: Australia. December Quarter 2017*. The Melbourne Institute, University of Melbourne.

Merriam-Webster. (2020). Poverty. In *Merriam-Webster.com dictionary*. Retrieved February 24, 2020, from www.merriam-webster.com/dictionary/poverty

Merton, R. K. (1968). *Social theory and social structure*. Simon and Schuster.

Mills, C. W. (1940). Situated actions and vocabularies of motive. *American Sociological Review, 5*, 904–913.

Misturelli, F., & Heffernan, C. (2012). The shape of change: A memetic analysis of the definitions of poverty from the 1970s to the 2000s. *Journal of International Development, 24*, S3–S18.

Mosse, D. (2010). A relational approach to durable poverty, inequality and power. *The Journal of Development Studies, 46*(7), 1156–1178. https://doi.org/10.1080/00220388.2010.487095

Nisbett, R. E., & Wilson, T. D. (1977). Telling more than we can know: Verbal reports on mental processes. *Psychological Review, 84*(3), 231.

Nussbaum, M. (2003). Capabilities as fundamental entitlements: Sen and social justice. *Feminist Economics, 9*(2–3), 33–59. https://doi.org/10.1080/1354570022000077926

Nussbaum, M. C. (2011). *Creating capabilities*. Harvard University Press.
Orshansky, M. (1963). Children of the poor. *Social Security Bulletin, 26*, 3.
Orshansky, M. (1965). Counting the poor: Another look at the poverty profile. *Social Security Bulletin, 28*, 3.
Orshansky, M. (1969). How poverty is measured. *Monthly Labor Review, 92*, 37.
Pettigrew, T. F. (2015). Samuel Stouffer and relative deprivation. *Social Psychology Quarterly, 78*(1), 7–24. https://doi.org/10.1177/0190272514566793
Polanyi, K. (1944/2001). *The great transformation: The political and economic origins of our time*. Beacon Press.
Potter, J., & Edwards, D. (1990). Nigel Lawson's tent: Discourse analysis, attribution theory and the social psychology of fact. *European Journal of Social Psychology, 20*, 405–424. https://doi.org/10.1002/ejsp.2420200504
Raphael, D. (2013). The politics of poverty: Definitions and explanations. *Social alternatives, 32*(1), 5.
Robeyns, I. (2005). The capability approach: A theoretical survey. *Journal of Human Development, 6*(1), 93–117. https://doi.org/10.1080/146498805200034266
Rowntree, B. S. (1901/1908). *Poverty, A study of town life*. MacMillan.
Runciman, W. G. (1966). *Relative deprivation & social justice: Study attitudes social inequality in 20th century England.* University of California Press.
Sánchez, E., Cronick, K., & Wiesenfeld, E. (2003). Poverty and community. In S . Carr & T . Sloan (eds.), *Poverty and psychology* (pp. 123–145). Springer.
Saunders, P., & Bedford, M. (2017). *New minimum income for healthy living budget standards for low-paid and unemployed Australians*. Social Policy Research Centre, University of New South Wales.
Saunders, P., Halleröd, B., & Matheson, G. (1994). Making ends meet in Australia and Sweden: A comparative analysis using the subjective poverty line methodology. *Acta Sociologica, 37*(1), 3–22. https://doi.org/10.1177/000169939403700101
Saunders, P., & Wilkins, R. (2016). Material deprivation. *The Household, Income and Labour Dynamics in Australia Survey: Selected Findings from Waves 1 to 14.* Melbourne Institute of Applied Economic and Social Research. ISSN 2205-0566 (Online).
Saunders, P., & Wong, M. (2008). *Deprivation and other indicators of the living standards of older Australians*. Social Policy Research Centre.
Scutella, R., Wilkins, R., & Kostenko, W. (2013). Intensity and persistence of individuals' social exclusion in Australia. *Australian Journal of Social Issues, 48*(3), 273–298. https://doi.org/10.1002/j.1839-4655.2013.tb00283.x
Sen, A. (1980). "Equality of what?". In McMurrin S *The Tanner lecture on human values, I* (pp. 197–220). Cambridge University Press.
Sen, A. (1983). Poor, relatively speaking. *Oxford Economic Papers, 35*(2), 153–169.
Sen, A. (1984). The living standard. *Oxford Economic Papers, 36*, 74–90.
Sen, A. (1985). A sociological approach to the measurement of poverty: A reply to Professor Peter Townsend. *Oxford Economic Papers, 37*(4), 669–676.
Sen, A. (1999). *Development as freedom*. Knopf.
Shelton, T. (2018). Rethinking the RECAP: Mapping the relational geographies of concentrated poverty and affluence in Lexington, Kentucky. *Urban Geography, 39*(7), 1070–1091. https://doi.org/10.1080/02723638.2018.1433927
Silver, H. (1994). Social exclusion and social solidarity: Three paradigms. *International Labour Review, 133*(5–6), 531–578.

Simmel, G. (1907/1971). *'Exchange'* [translated extract from Philosophie des Geldes. Leipzig, Duncker & Humbolt]. In G. Simmel (ed.), *On individuality and social form* (pp. 43–69). University of Chicago Press.
Smith, A. (1976/2007). An inquiry into the nature and causes of the wealth of nations. In E. Cannan (Ed.), Chicago: University of Chicago Press. (Original work published 1776).
Stouffer, S. A., Suchman, E. A., DeVinney, L. C., Starr, S. A., & Williams, R. M. (1949). *The American soldier: Adjustment to army life. (Studies in social psychology in World War II)*. Princeton University Press
Townsend, P. (1979). *Poverty in the United Kingdom: A survey of household resources and standards of living*. University of California Press.
Townsend, P. (1985). A sociological approach to the measurement of poverty—A rejoinder to Professor Amartya Sen. *Oxford Economic Papers, 37*(4), 659–668.
Townsend, P. (1993). Theoretical disputes about poverty. In P. Townsend (ed.). *The international analysis of poverty* (pp. 113–139). Routledge.
United Nations Development Programme (UNDP). (2018). *Human development indices and indicators: 2018 Statistical update*. United Nations Development Programme. Retrieved from https://hdr.undp.org/content/statistical-update-2018
Van den Bosch, K. (2001). *Identifying the poor: Using subjective and consensual measures*. Routledge.
Wagle, U. R. (2017). The politics of poverty measurement and social policies: Global observations. In R. White (ed.), *Measuring multidimensional poverty and deprivation: Incidence and determinants in developed countries* (pp. 7–30). Springer.
Walker, A., & Walker, C. (eds.) (1997). *Britain divided: The growth of social exclusion in the 1980s and 1990s*. CPAG.
Walker, R., Kyomuhendo, G. B., Chase, E., Choudhry, S., Gubrium, E. K., Nicola, J. Y., ... & Ming, Y. (2013). Poverty in global perspective: Is shame a common denominator? *Journal of Social Policy, 42*(2), 215–233. doi:10.1017/S0047279412000979
Weber, M. (1947/1964). *The theory of social and economic organization*. The Free Press.
White, R. (2017). *Measuring Multidimensional Poverty and Deprivation: Incidence and Determinants in Developed Countries*. Springer.
World Bank. (2016). *Poverty and shared prosperity 2016: Taking on inequality*. World Bank. doi:10.1596/978-1-4648-0958-3
Zelizer, V. (1995). *The social meaning of money*. Basic Books.
Zelizer, V. A. (2010). *Economic lives: How culture shapes the economy*. Princeton University Press.

3

PSYCHOLOGY OF POVERTY

Here comes the problem. The research I am reporting on was part of a PhD in psychology, so I had to have a chapter on the history of the psychology of poverty. Psychology, however, has, or is, often a tool to control people (Rose, 1988), particularly poor people, and psychology can be the primary means of finding the poor responsible for their poverty. The question psychology jumps over is:

> Is the issue/solution for poverty inside poor people or outside them in the world?

Psychology, to this point, has only been able to answer one way: inside them, but not for lack of trying. For those who have read previous books in this series, you would be aware of the fork in the road for psychology (Guerin, 2021). Psychology has mostly gone 'inside' to explain psychology by what the brain and mind do, but there is another option, turning it inside out and looking towards context. Historically, psychology has been the bastion for blaming the victim and I have been worried to see this still only paired with new discursive repertoires as if they solve the functional (political) issue of locating of poverty inside the poor. Which recursively is

> to believe that the poor are basically responsible for their poverty is also to exonerate economic and political institutions from that responsibility and to legitimize the efforts of authorities to change the poor person's attitudes and behavior.
>
> *(Edelman, 1998, p. 132)*

DOI: 10.4324/9781003453970-3

Psychological Explanations for Poverty

Psychology has always investigated topics that overlap with other disciplines. Yet, the field has had very little to say on economic behaviour despite money and economics being most of what we do in modern life (Carr & Sloan, 2003, p. 163; Guerin, 2003, p. 698; 2016, p. 86; Lea et al., 1987, p. xix; Rachlin, 1980, p. 212). To that end, psychological literature authors do not use a uniform measure of poverty. The most common way to identify the poor is, again, income. Recently 'subjective well-being' and personal identification as 'poor' have been included, along with some consideration of the time scales of poverty opposed to common "one-off" measurements (Adamkovič & Martončik, 2017, p. 2). Unfortunately, psychology has searched for and located the explanation, cause, or fault, of poverty consistently inside the poor (Carr, 2013; Turner & Lehning, 2007). Poverty is said to be a result of individual's personalities, attributions, and thinking that produce poverty-sustaining behaviour.

One of the earliest "psychological reductions" of poverty was Oscar Lewis' *Culture of Poverty* (Bourgois, 2001, p. 11905). Lewis, an anthropologist, suggested that parents instil problematic beliefs, attitudes, and behaviour patterns in their children which reproduce poverty (Bourgois, 2001; Lewis, 1959/1976). When the Culture of Poverty met politics, it was used against low-income African American families in the 1965 'Moynihan Report', suggesting Black Americans were to blame for their poverty (Bird, 2013; Bourgois, 2001).

The 'Moynihan Report' and the blaming rhetoric garnered widespread criticism, including from psychologists like William Ryan (1976), who coined the phrase 'blaming the victim' – a perennial issue by psychology for many topics (Edelman, 1998; Rappaport et al., 1975; Smail, 2001). The psychology of poverty still struggles with this as research on the disposition of the poor "become the basis for the victimization of the poor through creation of myths about them" (Tripathi, 2010, pp. 211–212). Researchers would not believe this is what their work does, including Oscar Lewis, who said of his 'culture of poverty', "There is nothing in the concept that puts the onus of poverty on the character of the poor" (Lewis, 1967, p. 499). Nevertheless, this is how the concept was used and has become its legacy (Bourgois, 2001). Keep this issue in mind throughout the next 50 years of research we are about to rush through.

Personality of the Poor

Using personality traits as an explanation for behaviour without context is a bigger psychological issue than I can critique (see Roberts, 2009) but it appears in the psychology of poverty too. One such theory from the 1960s was the finding that the poor had a low 'need for achievement': the poor were comfortable with achieving less compared to the non-poor (McClelland, 1961; Turner & Lehning, 2007). Maybe this was natural (biological) or maybe it was learned like a learned helplessness but nevertheless interventions for such a state would be to disrupt the behaviours and beliefs (cognitions) that maintain poverty.

Through the 1970s and 1980s (and still today), psychology has spent time attributing traits to the poor or the non-poor as two homogeneous groups. The poor are assumed to be psychologically different to the non-poor in several ways: a lower need for achievement (personality); external as compared to an internal locus of control – believing the world, not their own ability, controls outcomes; harmful just world beliefs – either believing they are the cause of their poverty or that they are unable to alter an unjust world; and negative self-concept such as blaming oneself for their position (Furnham, 2003, pp. 165–166). These ways of thinking and behaving are often treated as innate, biological, and heritable and since the 1980s, an increase in individualising the issue of poverty, in Western nations, has continued. At the same time, an internal individualisation accompanies the suggestion that contextual reasons for poverty are all but solved (at least in the Western world):

> In the absence of prohibitive barriers to employment, the question of the personality of the poor emerges as the key to understanding and overcoming poverty. Psychology is the last frontier in the search for the causes of low work effort.
>
> *(Mead, 1986, p. 133)*

The implication is that poverty is a result of poor disposition, personality, or learnt behaviour that stops people working and striving for a good life. Such suggestions have continued through to today (e.g., P. R. Saunders, 2004; also see critiques in Klein, 2016; Phelan, 2014). At the same time opposition victim blaming was present in mainstream psychological research.

Attributing the Cause of Poverty

Social psychology rather than look at the explicit cause of poverty examined what different social groups *think the cause of poverty is*. 'Attributional' research produced an immense amount of literature on how people attribute blame for poverty, continuing to today (Da Costa & Dias, 2014; Davis & Reyna, 2015; Kornbluh et al., 2019; Mickelson & Hazlett, 2014; Piff et al., 2020).

Generally, the causal attributions of poverty are separated along a set of three broad categories set out by Feagin (1972): individualistic – the person's fault; structural – the society's fault; or fatalistic – luck based. While people can stick with one attribution over time, the explanations are not always "internally coherent" (Furnham, 2003, p. 182). Different attributions correlate with age, education, and religion, among other variables. There are interconnected beliefs about the causes of poverty, causes of wealth, and causes of unemployment that link to political ideology. Put simply, "left-wing people (and postmaterialists) are more inclined to attribute poverty to social causes, whereas the right wing are more likely to blame the victims" (Furnham, 2003, p. 171). Those attributions are related to voting behaviour and charitable behaviour. One issue is that correlations do not explain why and how these links occur and require more direct observation of processes that connect these findings (Furnham, 2003, p. 167). These findings are a piece in explaining behaviour towards the poor but not poverty itself.

Discursive Critique of Attributional Research

Attributional research has been popular and reveal some of the information we need but there is more to consider. Harper (1996, 2003) directly criticised such research for a lack of context and *functionality* of attributions. Harper questioned the usefulness of attributional data in several ways. First, we focus on the most common (average) response of a group rather than the reason for a certain attribution. Second, we assume these are stable across contexts. Third, we ask in surveys only allowing people to pick one of several options offered by the researchers. Harper suggest that we need to examine the whole system maintaining poverty, rather than the most common attribution used in a social group.

Harper warned if we treat people's talking about poverty as the actual psychology of poverty we may be falling into the same trap as before:

> Whilst most psychologists and other social scientists no longer engage in "blaming the victim" (Ryan, 1971), in the overt ways which Pearl (1970) documents, they continue to do so indirectly.
>
> *(Harper, 2003, p. 188)*

To understand the systems that maintain poverty "it would be important to explore the public explanations and images of poverty" but only as they function to maintain poverty not as truth of how people in poverty are (Harper, 1996, p. 262). Attribution is something we do when talking to others, and the poor can react and resist blame for their poverty (Scott, 1990). Again, the relational level of poverty is coming into focus. With attribution we can investigate ways people relate to, and reproduce, the contexts of or for creating poverty (Hodgetts & Stolte, 2017, pp. 2–3; Hodgetts et al., 2019).

Cognitive Feedback Loop

Cognitive psychology uses models of information processing to represent what is carried out by the human mind. The models usually include the intake, storage, retrieval, and use of information by the brain, used to decide on and produce behaviour. The relation of such models to poverty comes from if these internal cognitive systems err and produce dysfunctional behaviours that may result in poverty. These mistakes, however, are neither the individual nor from their social and political barriers but natural biological limitations of the brain common amongst all humans (Anand & Lea, 2011; Bertrand et al., 2004; Mani et al., 2013).

One popular explanation for poverty behaviours is a feedback loop. All people have natural, biological, limited 'cognitive bandwidth', 'cognitive resources', or capacity for 'cognitive load'. The stress and negative affect caused by poverty produce an increase in cognitive 'load', and when the 'bandwidth' or 'resources' are exhausted, this leads to decreases in executive functioning, including willpower, self-control, working memory, and attention. An article titled 'Poverty Impedes Cognitive Function' by Mani et al. (2013) had notable presence in public media as journalists picked up on the phrase "the effects we observed correspond to ~13 IQ points" (p. 980). That phrase was translated to: "How poverty can drive down intelligence" (Solman, 2018) and "Poverty changes your brain to make you less intelligent, study suggests" (Johnston, 2016). Despite this popularity, the claims have been extremely well critiqued elsewhere as the foundations have too many holes (Dang et al., 2015), or that poverty itself was not part of the measures (Wicherts & Scholten, 2013). These do nothing to the impact of the idea that poor people's intelligence is a cause of poverty.

Cognitive declines are observed as poor economic decisions, more technically described as a movement from "goal-directed to habitual behaviour" (Haushofer & Fehr, 2014, p. 866; Adamkovič & Martončik, 2017). This habitual behaviour is irrational because the outcome would be better if the poor had chosen another option and that choice, therefore, maintains poverty. Poverty then continues, stress increases or remains at a detrimental level, and feeds back to create decreased cognitive ability.

Habitual behaviour is behaviour learned to the point that it becomes a simple and automatic response in which no 'thinking' occurs (Adams, 1982; Balleine & Dickinson, 1991; Dickinson, 1985; Schwabe, & Wolf, 2009). So, the claim is the poor do not consider consequences before they act. In the case of monetary poverty, the poor *time-discount*: choose to take small amounts of money sooner over large amounts of money later. The poor are also *risk-averse*: will risk large losses if there is a chance of no losses in the hope of losing nothing, and conversely will take small gains over gambling bigger gains. These choices are economically irrational, as waiting a short time for bigger rewards is 'better' from a rational perspective, and the mathematics of the risk is in favour of gambling those losses. These choices are said to be evidence of an 'intuitive thinking style' or 'system one', a fast, implicit, and heuristics-based cognitive system, as compared to the 'deliberative system' or 'system two', which is slower, rational, and logical (Kahneman, 2011).

This model attributes the outcome (poverty) *almost exclusively* to internal, mental, cognitive systems. The factors, which could be considered external, are stress and the effect of financial literacy – knowledge of finance and economics. Financial literacy is a moderating factor for the results of time-discounting and risk-aversion (Adamkovič & Martončik, 2017, p. 7). This literacy, described as knowledge, beliefs, and attitudes about financial management, is considered in terms of education, and is linked to social structures of disadvantage. The reasoning behind separating financial literacy from cognitive resources, which include expertise and knowledge, is potentially due to financial literacy being poor throughout all societies and, therefore, not easily considered an individual deficit (Wolf, 2018).

So, cognitive psychology describes the poor as people who, due to stress, suffer from reduced cognitive ability, leading to poverty-maintaining behaviours. How does cognitive psychology suggest we address this feedback loop? One answer is individual-level 'psychological interventions' (Haushofer & Fehr, 2014, p. 866; Adamkovič & Martončik, 2017, p. 10). Haushofer and Fehr's (2014) review contains various prospective intervention points, such as unconditional cash transfers, help changing job status, and possibly psychotherapy for the poor's mental well-being to improve their economic behaviour.

What the Poor Are Risking, and What Stresses Them Out

The implication is that habitual behaviour are the poor making errors. Such inferences are somewhat benign, the maths says it is irrational. It would not be a problem if these claims did not accompany dispositional ascriptions. Unfortunately, when we read reviews such as Adamkovič and Martončik's (2017) the disposition of the poor reappears as the culprit. For example, thinking things through (system two) means to "do it if it makes sense" while acting quickly (system one) is the "do it if it feels good" system (p. 5 citing de Ridder et al., 2012, p. 78). Or: "It appears evident that poor people **favor** immediate and smaller rewards that provide short-term **satisfaction** but are not economically beneficial from the long-term perspective" (p. 6, emphasis added). Similarly, "Are people living in poverty **more eager** to accept the certainty of a smaller reward or might they **willingly** take the risk of losing a potential bigger reward?" (p. 6, emphasis added). The implication is that the poor who remain poor are trying to feel good, but feelings, desire, want, satisfaction, favour, eagerness, and willingness of participants are not part of the data, instead these are added in as conclusions.

Haushofer and Fehr's (2014) review assessed 'happiness' and mental illness statistics as they correlated with wealth, finding the poor much less happy and more mentally ill. But again, the poor were "hedonistic", seeking "instant gratification" (p. 9). Such concepts conflate a lack of self-control with a wish for pleasure while these people are otherwise suffering. The poor are often 'not happy', but their error is when they seek small gratification or pleasure: the solution is to teach them to go longer without gratification. To be clear, the behavioural data is not in dispute here, the measure show the poor are more risk-averse and time-discount compared to non-poor populations. What I do question is the generation of a theory with internal assumptions without checking what motivates these behaviours in context. Are poor people really seeking out hedonistic happiness to alleviate their suffering or are there other goals?

Take note of the year; and think about the victim blaming of the 1960s. Haushofer and Fehr (2014) are aware of this stating "dysfunctional institutions, exposure to violence and crime, poor access to health care, and a host of other obstacles and inconveniences" (p. 862) that lead to poverty. They also begin their investigation with a caveat.

> Second, in asking whether poverty reinforces itself through psychological channels, we are not suggesting that the poor bear blame for their poverty. Rather, an environment of poverty into which one happens to have been born can trigger processes that reinforce poverty. On this view, any one of us might be poor if it were not for certain environmental coincidences.
>
> *(p. 862)*

Like Oscar Lewis before, the character of the poor is not to blame, and I am sure this is genuinely intended but reading these points back-to-back begs if we have other ways of working with people experiencing poverty which better incorporate the praxis of these caveats to not require them at all.

Also confusing is what we mean by 'stress'. The stress of poverty is various; just read the big lists of missing experiences and resources spoken about in Chapter 2, so this must be the stress that is studied for the feedback loop: right?

Adamkovič and Martončik's (2017) review includes ten studies on stress's effect on cognition. The studies 'stress induction' mechanisms include putting the participants hand in ice water (Porcelli & Delgado, 2009, p. 279), difficult mathematics tasks (Braunstein-Bercovitz, 2003, p. 348; Haushofer & Shapiro, 2013, p. 2; Moreno, 2015, pp. iv–v), and social interactions like a fake job interview or presentation (Haushofer & Shapiro, 2013, p. 2; Moreno, 2015, pp. iv–v; Simonovic et al., 2016, p. 659). The measures for stress ranged from 7-point self-report scales to full interviews with full biological tests for allostatic load and cortisol levels. My question is how those stress tasks are at all comparable to poverty's often chronic (or churning) stressors for basic human needs. This harkens back to critiques of social psychology in the 1960–1980s (Faye, 2012), where experimental designs did not at all compare to the reality and the context they wish to describe. Using these experimental findings imply a hand in ice water is like the stress of poverty because these are the data we draw for these claims.

My critiques are rather nit-picky compared to others' issues with the feedback loop. Another review criticised the assumption that intuitive or fast thinking is worse than deliberative thinking; Yu (2016, p. 92) instead says the usefulness of a thinking style depends on context. Other studies pointed out the difference in chronic to acute stress, mainly that chronic stress flattens the effect of cortisol and that previous research and theory suggest stress can be both good and bad depending on context (Mather & Lighthall, 2012, p. 40; Starcke & Brand, 2012, p. 1243). We need a better understanding of stress in poverty. We cannot rely on a theory that studies stress, worries, thinking in ways that make only the poor responsible for their faults, no matter how many caveats we use in justifying that research.

Behavioural Economics' Nudge Intervention

Psychology rarely recognises economics itself, but economics often incorporates psychological concepts to support theories, apparently regardless of the validity and accuracy of those concepts (see Zafirovski, 2005). But today behavioural economics has been influential, two proponents garnering Nobel prizes in economics (Daniel Kahneman and Richard Thaler). The area has a long history of using behavioural data to generate cognitive theories of economic behaviour and uncovering cognitive biases and heuristics.

Economics, in some forms, assumes that humans are rational: picking the best option for themselves mathematically and logically. Behavioural economics, a subdiscipline of economics, rejects that assumption in favour of bounded rationality. Bounded rationality means people will act irrationally because information is low or *cognitive heuristics* lead to choices for less than the best option (Simon, 1972). Those behaviours/choices are still often labelled errors or mistakes (see Kahneman, 2003, p. 1406; Levine, 2011, pp. 293, 300; Martinez & Zeelenberg, 2015, p. 120; Sunstein, 2017, p. x). Behavioural economics allows such mistakes to be understood as rational under certain conditions or contexts (Soukup et al., 2015, p. 8).

Behavioural economics uses psychological theories about cognitive biases and heuristics, particularly that of Prospect Theory, which explains how people make choices with risk and uncertainty (Tversky & Kahneman, 1979). More recently, these veins of thought have developed into a general theory of human thinking (Kahneman, 2011), benefits to irrationalities (Ariely, 2008), and policy-based interventions for when "humans predictably err" (Thaler

& Sunstein, 2008, p. 8). Remember, however, that the poor's errors are not unique to the poor as all humans are irrational, but it is costlier in poor contexts.

Thaler and Sunstein's (2008) book, *Nudge: Improving decisions about health, wealth, and happiness*, describes behaviour economic intervention. 'Nudge' theory is set out under "Libertarian Paternalism" (p. 5) providing freedom by guidance, with acknowledgment of the contradictory meanings. The aim is to improve the choices made by the public regarding economics and health by altering the available information or effort needed to undertake certain options to limit the chance of errors. "Choice architects" make subtle but effective changes to the world to encourage healthier or more rational economic choices.

Most of these changes are "harmless" and effortless; for example, in a cafeteria "motivating" healthier eating by making healthy food more physically accessible (at eye level, with clearer pricing and information) as compared to unhealthy food (Thaler & Sunstein, 2008, pp. 1–3). In other cases, using opt-out rather than opt-in systems increases participation in social programmes; for example, using an opt-out system for organ donation increases donation (2008, pp. 175–182). Behavioural economics has much more to say on the influence of biases and heuristics in generating irrational behaviour. The main point here is to show how cognitive theories entangle with behavioural economics and how these theories have now spawned influential perspectives on dealing with the irrational economic behaviour of the general population and by virtue the poor.

Critiquing the Assumptions of Behavioural Economics

The ideological position of behavioural economics, particularly the paternalistic element, align to policies of 'mutual obligation' welfare systems present and active in Australia (Bradbury et al., 2013, p. 263; Curchin, 2017; Standing, 2011b, p. 27). These policies are aimed to help the poor make better choices for their economic future. The assumption is that people benefit from optimal self-focused effort ('utility maximising' sometimes selfishly). People do not act this way though, and sometimes this is marked as irrational. People pick other options for many reasons, but behavioural economics has kept some of these old assumptions and concepts active in the judgement of behaviour – people would be rational if not for heuristics and limited information (Levine et al., 2015; Rachlin, 2015; Zafirovski, 2005, p. 5).

Again, people make unhealthy, or irrational economic choices, by acting "mindlessly" (Thaler & Sunstein, 2008, pp. 38, 40, 44, 46–47). The poor, and poverty, are spoken of sparingly in *Nudge*. Everyone is said to commit the same errors, but it remains that the cause of poor economic choices is internal, thinking, deficits. When the poor are spoken of it is framed in a certain way: discussing mortgage brokerage "the poor are often fleeced by people pretending to be providing a service" (p. 134). Another section wants to allay worries people have about redistribution to "benefit the weak, poor, uneducated, or unsophisticated" by stating that Nudges aim only to help poor people at a "minimal cost" to others (pp. 241–242). Nudge also questions "how much learning [from mistakes] is good for people?" (p. 241). The assistance to these people is given more time than a critique of the above predation. Interventions rest on the idea being bad at rational thinking means we must be encouraged to improve. The focus is not morally corrupt individuals but individuals performing poorly due to natural limitations. The implication is that the location of the fault, or cause, is still the person who is "fleeced", acting "mindlessly", or is "the weak, poor, uneducated, or unsophisticated".

The issue is not that nudges do not work, the issue is with the assumptions that underlie what is considered right and wrong, correct and mistake. Rachlin (2015, p. 200), criticising nudge, draws out this point saying, "who will control the controllers?", as does Standing (2011a, pp. 238–242, 2011b). More pointedly: are we defining rational as healthy and happy or delaying gratification and having more money? Or: for what other reasons do people make these 'wrong'/'mistaken' economic choices?

In fact, serious criticism of the usefulness, and even morality, for nudge interventions and above foundations have been raised. This chapter is an overview though, not a critique of these interventions which others have done so well (see Bissonnette, 2016; Bradbury et al., 2013; Curchin, 2017; Leggett, 2014; Rachlin, 2015; Standing, 2011b). The key point here is that psychological explanation still locates the issue inside people despite 60+ years of accepting it is problematic and not the whole picture.

Contextual Psychology of Poverty

What are those other reasons that people choose 'irrational' options? Henrich et al. (2001, p. 77) spoke to participants who rejected rational 'positive offers' in the ultimatum game; it was not an error, they had goals other than maximising payoff. Henrich and colleagues (2001) say that fairness, reciprocity, changing material outcomes, and cooperation were important. Readers of this series will note that these other reasons are some of the core social contextual behaviours that need explaining (Guerin, 2016). Even Simon (1972), writing about bounded rationality, wrote that "conditions and constraints" are found "in the environment, outside the skin of the rational actor" (p. 162).

Much of the psychology of poverty pays lip service to the idea of context outside the actor. For example, de Ridder et al. (2012), in their meta-analysis of 'self-control', found that self-control is positively correlated to desired behaviours and negatively correlated to undesired behaviours: "Whether behavior is regarded as desirable or undesirable is thus highly influenced by contextual factors and may even be idiosyncratic as it relates to the personal goals an individual holds" (p. 79). To avoid the complicating issue of 'idiosyncratic contextual factors' the authors define desired behaviour as generalised responsibilities, duties, and obligations that adhere to 'social norms'. Desired behaviours follow social norms, improve happiness, success, and health. The undesirable is antisocial, destructively impulsive, to be absent, to overeat, or to have conflict. But these undesirable things are often the tools of agitation by the disadvantaged. This separation between rational and 'irrational', desired and undesired, or whatever dichotomy you like, must not identify that which is comfortable for the status quo if we want to change economic outcomes for large groups. The dichotomy is really 'social and rational' not 'irrational and rational' (Guerin, 2020). The issue may be as Richardson et al. (2018) argued, "psychologists [are] underequipped ... to speak of socio-political and economic matters" (p. 17).

There are, and have been, psychological perspectives that by design will not locate the feedback loops in the poor's cognition, dispositions, beliefs, attitudes, or personalities, nor by predictable irrationalities but rather as emergent with context, given that "Behavior is actually, typically, a function of interactions between people and their environments" (Carr, 2013, p. 15; Lewin, 1936 [B = f(P, E)]; Skinner, 1974 [radical behaviourism]; Guerin, 2016, 2021 [contextual analysis]; Hodgetts & Stolte, 2017 [relational approach to urban poverty]). These different forms of explaining behaviour bolster the criticisms above and highlight the need for better descriptions of the contexts, stressors, behaviours, and actual goals of poor people.

References

Adamkovič, M., & Martončik, M. (2017). A review of consequences of poverty on economic decision-making: A hypothesized model of a cognitive mechanism. *Frontiers in Psychology, 8*, 1784. https://doi.org/10.3389/fpsyg.2017.01784

Adams, C. D. (1982). Variations in the sensitivity of instrumental responding to reinforcer devaluation. *The Quarterly Journal of Experimental Psychology Section B, 34*(2b), 77–98. https://doi.org/10.1080/14640748208400878

Anand, P., & Lea, S. (2011). The psychology and behavioural economics of poverty. *Journal of Economic Psychology, 32*(2), 284–293. https://doi.org/10.1016/j.joep.2010.11.004

Ariely, D. (2008) *Predictably irrational*. Harper Collins.

Balleine, B., & Dickinson, A. (1991). Instrumental performance following reinforcer devaluation depends upon incentive learning. *The Quarterly Journal of Experimental Psychology, 43*(3), 279–296.

Bertrand, M., Mullainathan, S., & Shafir, E. (2004). A behavioral-economics view of poverty. *American Economic Review, 94*(2), 419–423. doi:10.1257/0002828041302019

Bird, K. (2013). The intergenerational transmission of poverty: An overview. In A. Shepard & J. Brunt (Eds.), *Chronic poverty* (pp. 60–84). Palgrave Macmillan.

Bissonnette, J. F. (2016). From the moral to the neural: Brain scans, decision-making, and the problematization of economic (ir) rationality. *Journal of Cultural Economy, 9*(4), 364–381. doi:10.1080/17530350.2016.1181097

Bourgois, P. (2001). Culture of poverty. In: N. J. Smelser & P. B. Baltes, (Eds.), *International encyclopedia of the social & behavioral sciences* (pp. 11904–11907). Waveland Press. http://dx.doi.org/10.1016/B0-08-043076-7/00841-X

Bradbury, A., McGimpsey, I., & Santori, D. (2013). Revising rationality: The use of 'Nudge' approaches in neoliberal education policy. *Journal of Education Policy, 28*(2), 247–267. doi:10.1080/02680939.2012.719638

Braunstein-Bercovitz, H. (2003). Does stress enhance or impair selective attention? The effects of stress and perceptual load on negative priming. *Anxiety, Stress, and Coping, 16*(4), 345–357. https://doi.org/10.1080/1061580031000112560

Carr, S. C. (2013). *Anti-poverty psychology*. Springer Science & Business Media.

Carr, S. C., & Sloan, T. (eds.). (2003). *Poverty and psychology: From global perspective to local practice*. Springer Science & Business Media.

Curchin, K. (2017). Using behavioural insights to argue for a stronger social safety net: Beyond libertarian paternalism. *Journal of Social Policy, 46*(2), 231–249. doi:10.1017/S0047279416000672

Da Costa, L. P., & Dias, J. G. (2014). Perceptions of poverty attributions in Europe: A multilevel mixture model approach. *Quality & Quantity, 48*(3), 1409–1419. https://doi.org/10.1007/s11135-013-9843-3

Dang, J., Xiao, S., & Dewitte, S. (2015). Commentary: "Poverty impedes cognitive function" and "The poor's poor mental power". *Frontiers in Psychology, 6*, 1037. https://doi.org/10.3389/fpsyg.2015.01037

Davis, J. R., & Reyna, C. (2015). Seeing red: How perceptions of social status and worth influence hostile attributions and endorsement of aggression. *British Journal of Social Psychology, 54*(4), 728–747. doi:10.1111/bjso.12109

De Ridder, D. T., Lensvelt-Mulders, G., Finkenauer, C., Stok, F. M., & Baumeister, R. F. (2012). Taking stock of self-control: A meta-analysis of how trait self-control relates to a wide range of behaviors. *Personality and Social Psychology Review, 16*(1), 76–99. https://doi.org/10.1177/1088868311418749

Dickinson, A. (1985). Actions and habits: The development of behavioural autonomy. *Philosophical Transactions of the Royal Society of London. B, Biological Sciences, 308*(1135), 67–78. https://doi.org/10.1098/rstb.1985.0010

Edelman, M. (1998). Language, myths and rhetoric. *Society, 35*(2), 131–139. https://doi.org/10.1007/BF02838136

Faye, C. (2012). American social psychology: Examining the contours of the 1970s crisis. *Studies in History and Philosophy of Biological and Biomedical Sciences, 43*(2), 514–521. https://doi.org/10.1016/j.shpsc.2011.11.010

Feagin, J. R. (1972). Poverty: We still believe that God helps those who help themselves. *Psychology Today, 6*(6), 101–110.

Furnham, A. (2003). Poverty and wealth. In S . Carr & T . Sloan (eds.), *Poverty and psychology* (pp. 163–184). Springer.

Guerin, B. (2003). Putting a radical socialness into consumer behavior analysis. *Journal of Economic Psychology, 24*(5), 697–718. https://doi.org/10.1016/S0167-4870(03)00009-6

Guerin, B. (2016). *How to rethink human behavior: A practical guide to social contextual analysis*. Routledge.

Guerin, B. (2020). *Turning psychology into a social science*. Routledge.

Guerin, B. (2021). *Turning psychology into social contextual analysis*. Routledge.

Harper, D. J. (1996). Accounting for poverty: From attribution to discourse. *Journal of Community & Applied Social Psychology, 6*(4), 249–265. https://doi.org/10.1007/978-1-4615-0029-2_10

Harper, D. J. (2003). Poverty and discourse. In S . Carr & T . Sloan (eds.), *Poverty and psychology* (pp. 185–204). Springer.
Haushofer, J., & Fehr, E. (2014). On the psychology of poverty. *Science, 344*(6186), 862–867. doi:10.1126/science.1232491
Haushofer, J., & Shapiro, J. (2013). Household response to income changes: Evidence from an unconditional cash transfer program in Kenya. *Massachusetts Institute of Technology, 24*(5), 1–57. Available at http://web.mit.edu/joha/www/publications/haushofer_shapiro_uct_2013.11.16.pdf
Henrich, J., Boyd, R., Bowles, S., Camerer, C., Fehr, E.. Gintis, H., & McElreath, R. (2001). In search of homo economicus: Behavioral experiments in 15 small-scale societies. *American Economic Review, 91*(2), 73–78. doi:10.1257/aer.91.2.73
Hodgetts, D., & Stolte, O. (2017) *Urban poverty and health inequalities: A relational approach*. Routledge.
Hodgetts, D., Stolte, O., King, P., & Groot, S. (2019). Reproducing the general through the local: Lessons from poverty research. In C. Højholt & E. Schraube (eds.), *Subjectivity and knowledge* (pp. 157–174). Springer. https://doi.org/10.1007/978-3-030-29977-4
Johnston, I. (2016). Poverty changes your brain to make you less intelligent, study suggests. *Independent*. www.independent.co.uk/news/science/poverty-intelligence-aging-brain-low-income-inequality-a7333506.html
Kahneman, D. (2003). Maps of bounded rationality: Psychology for behavioral economics. *American Economic Review, 93*(5), 1449–1475. DOI: 10.1257/000282803322655392
Kahneman, D. (2011). *Thinking, fast and slow*. Macmillan.
Klein, E. (2016). Neoliberal subjectivities and the behavioural focus on income management. *Australian Journal of Social Issues, 51*(4), 503–523. https://doi.org/10.1002/j.1839-4655.2016.tb01246.x
Kornbluh, M. E., Pykett, A. A., & Flanagan, C. A. (2019). Exploring the associations between youths' explanations of poverty at the societal level and judgements of distributive justice. *Developmental Psychology, 55*(3), 488–497. https://doi.org/10.1037/dev0000523
Lea, S. E., Tarpy, R. M., & Webley, P. M. (1987). *The individual in the economy: A textbook of economic psychology*. CUP Archive.
Leggett, W. (2014). The politics of behaviour change: Nudge, neoliberalism and the state. *Policy & Politics, 42*(1), 3–19. http://dx.doi.org/10.1332/030557312X655576
Levine, D. K. (2011). Neuroeconomics?. *International Review of Economics, 58*(3), 287. doi:10.1007/s12232-011-0128-7
Levine, J., Chan, K. M., & Satterfield, T. (2015). From rational actor to efficient complexity manager: Exorcising the ghost of Homo economicus with a unified synthesis of cognition research. *Ecological Economics, 114*, 22–32. http://dx.doi.org/10.1016/j.ecolecon.2015.03.010
Lewin, K. (1936). *Principles of topographical psychology*. (F. Heider, G. Heider Trans.). McGraw Book Company.
Lewis, O. (1967). The children of Sanchez—Autobiography of a Mexican family. *Current Anthropology, 8*, 480–500.
Lewis, O. (1959/1976). *Five families: Mexican case studies in the culture of poverty*. Souvenir Press.
Mani, A., Mullainathan, S., Shafir, E., & Zhao, J. (2013). Poverty impedes cognitive function. *Science, 341*(6149), 976–980.

Martinez, L. F., & Zeelenberg, M. (2015). Trust me (or not): Regret and disappointment in experimental economic games. *Decision, 2*(2), 118. http://dx.doi.org/10.1037/dec0000025

Mather, M., & Lighthall, N. R. (2012). Risk and reward are processed differently in decisions made under stress. *Current Directions in Psychological Science, 21*(1), 36–41. https://doi.org/10.1177/0963721411429452

McClelland, D. C. (1961). *The achieving society*. Van Nostrand.

Mead, L. M. (1986). *Beyond entitlement: The social obligations of citizenship*. Free Press.

Mickelson, K. D., & Hazlett, E. (2014). "Why me?": Low-income women's poverty attributions, mental health, and social class perceptions. *Sex Roles, 71*(9–10), 319–332. doi:10.1007/s11199-014-0414-4

Moreno, G. L. (2015). *The effects of stress on decision making and the prefrontal cortex among older adults*. Ph.D. dissertation, University of Iowa, Iowa City, IA.

Piff, P. K., Wiwad, D., Robinson, A. R., Aknin, L. B., Mercier, B., & Shariff, A. (2020). Shifting attributions for poverty motivates opposition to inequality and enhances egalitarianism. *Nature Human Behaviour, 4*(5), 496–505. https://doi.org/10.1038/s41562-020-0835-8

Phelan, S. (2014). *Neoliberalism, media and the political*. Springer.

Porcelli, A. J., & Delgado, M. R. (2009). Acute stress modulates risk taking in financial decision making. *Psychological Science, 20*(3), 278–283. https://doi.org/10.1111/j.1467-9280.2009.02288.x

Rachlin, H. (1980). Economics and behavioral psychology. In J. E. R. Staddon (ed.), *Limits to action: The allocation of individual behavior* (pp. 205–236). Academic Press.

Rachlin, H. (2015). Choice architecture: A review of why nudge: The politics of libertarian paternalism. *Journal of the Experimental Analysis of Behavior, 104*(2), 198–203. https://doi.org/10.1002/jeab.163

Rappaport, J., Davidson, W. S., Wilson, M. N., & Mitchell, A. (1975). Alternatives to blaming the victim or the environment: Our places to stand have not moved the earth. *American Psychologist, 30*(4), 525–528. https://doi.org/10.1037/h0078449

Richardson, F. C., Bishop, R. C., & Garcia-Joslin, J. (2018). Overcoming neoliberalism. *Journal of Theoretical and Philosophical Psychology, 38*(1), 15. http://dx.doi.org/10.1037/teo0000071

Roberts, B. W. (2009). Back to the future: *Personality and Assessment* and personality development. *Journal of Research in Personality, 43*(2), 137–145. https://doi.org/10.1016/j.jrp.2008.12.015

Rose, N. (1988). Calculable minds and manageable individuals. *History of the Human Sciences, 1*(2), 179–200. https://doi.org/10.1177/095269518800100202

Ryan, W. (1976). *Blaming the victim* (Rev. updated). Vintage Books.

Saunders, P. R. (2004). *Australia's welfare habit and how to kick it*. Duffy & Snellgrove Centre for Independent Studies.

Schwabe, L., & Wolf, O. T. (2009). Stress prompts habit behavior in humans. *Journal of Neuroscience, 29*(22), 7191–7198. https://doi.org/10.1523/JNEUROSCI.0979-09.2009

Scott, J. C. (1990). *Domination and the arts of resistance: Hidden transcripts*. Yale University Press.

Simon, H. A. (1972). Theories of bounded rationality. In C. B. McGuire & R. Radner (eds.), *Decision and organization* (pp. 161–176). North Holland Publishing Company.

Simonovic, B., Stupple, E. J., Gale, M., & Sheffield, D. (2016). Stress and risky decision making: Cognitive reflection, emotional learning or both. *Journal of Behavioral Decision Making, 30*(2), 658–665. doi:10.1002/bdm.1980

Skinner, B. F. (1974). *About behaviorism.* Alfred A Knopf.

Smail, D. (2001). De-psychologizing community psychology. *Journal of Community and Applied Social Psychology, 11*, 159–165. https://doi.org/10.1002/casp.621

Solman, P. (2018). Analysis: How poverty can drive down intelligence. *PBS – Making Sen$e.* www.pbs.org/newshour/economy/making-sense/analysis-how-poverty-can-drive-down-intelligence

Soukup, A., Maitah, M., & Svoboda, R. (2015). The concept of rationality in neoclassical and behavioural economic theory. *Modern Applied Science, 9*(3), 1.

Standing, G. (2011a). *The precariat: The new dangerous class.* Bloomsbury Academic.

Standing, G. (2011b). Behavioural conditionality: Why the nudges must be stopped-an opinion piece. *Journal of Poverty and Social Justice, 19*(1), 27–38. https://doi.org/10.1332/175982711X559136

Starcke, K., & Brand, M. (2012). Decision making under stress: A selective review. *Neuroscience & Biobehavioral Reviews, 36*(4), 1228–1248. https://doi.org/10.1016/j.neubiorev.2012.02.003

Sunstein, C. R. (2017). Introduction "don't tell me what I can't do!": On the intrinsic value of control. In A. Samson (ed.), *The behavioural economics guide 2017* (pp. v–xiii). Retrieved from www.behavioraleconomics.com

Thaler, R. H., & Sunstein, C. R. (2008). *Nudge improving decisions about health, wealth, and happiness.* Yale University Press.

Tripathi, R. C. (2010). Poverty alleviation: Is it only tiling at the windmills? Introduction to Special Issue. *Psychology and Developing Societies, 22*(2), 201–220. doi:10.1177/097133361002200201

Turner, K., & Lehning, A. J. (2007). Psychological theories of poverty. *Journal of Human Behavior in the Social Environment, 16*(1–2), 57–72. doi:10.1300/J137v16n01_05

Tversky, A., & Kahneman, D. (1979). Prospect theory: An analysis of decision under risk. *Econometrica, 47*(2), 263–291.

Wicherts, J. M., & Scholten, A. Z. (2013). Comment on "Poverty impedes cognitive function". *Science (New York, N.Y.), 342*(6163), 1169. https://doi.org/10.1126/science.1246680

Wolf, M. (2018). Ain't misbehaving: Behavioral economics and the making of financial literacy. *Economic Sociology – The European Electronic Newsletter, 19*(2), 10–18.

Yu, R. (2016). Stress potentiates decision biases: A stress induced deliberation-to-intuition (SIDI) model. *Neurobiology of Stress, 3*, 83–95. https://doi.org/10.1016/j.ynstr.2015.12.006

Zafirovski, M. (2005). Social exchange theory under scrutiny: A positive critique of its economic-behaviorist formulations. *Electronic Journal of Sociology, 2*(2), 1–40.

4

THE CONTEXTS OF POVERTY

There is a choice in presenting the contexts of poverty. I could present all the theories and explanations of poverty in sociology and anthropology, but that is still an academic choosing what is most important. So, instead we will explore the contexts reported by poor people in academic literature. Privileging the voice of the poor seems prudent.

I completed a review for my PhD (Thain, 2020) which examined literature fitting these limitations:

- included experiences of any of the different concepts of poverty.
- spoke about people's lives not just their feelings.
- was published since 2003.
- was in English (because of my limitations).
- represented a metropolitan Western liberal welfare economy like Australia (i.e., the United States, Canada, Ireland, and the UK).

I focused on context not only because I was trained in social contextual analysis, but that it seemed prudent for poverty research in psychology:

> we are encouraged to focus on what is wrong with poor people, and on their bad decisions, rather than on what might be wrong with the context in which those decisions have to be made.
>
> *(Peel, 2003, p. 23)*

I read hundreds of articles and several books. In the end, 88 texts I collected matched the above criteria, 29 Australian articles and two books and 59 international texts. A lot of discarded research did not quote their participants

DOI: 10.4324/9781003453970-4

which I considered necessary, otherwise, were too focused in on one issue or were far too broad. For example, the book *Poverty* by Ruth Lister (2004) is informative and insightful but is largely a discussion of the concepts and their applicability to the UK – an amazing book to read for more real conversation on what the concepts of poverty mean.

Just as psychology consistently finds causes in the poor, qualitative poverty research of the social sciences finds consistent contexts. With every addition was the repetition, that poverty is an issue of policy, of bad work, of limited education. There was a "rediscovery of old news" (Carr, 2013, p. 4). Still, I want to set out those often-discovered contexts.

Neoliberalism as the Backdrop for Psychology and Poverty

Raewyn Connell describes neoliberalism as the backdrop life plays out against, like fascism in the early 1900s (2010, p. 24). We live and breathe it. Neoliberalism is, however, a nebulous term. To reduce the concept too much, *neoliberalism is an ideology, made real through policy and practice, concerned with the freedom, or rather liberation, of the individual, by seeking to make each person responsible for their life in its' entirety* (see Phelan, 2014, p. 57; Wacquant, 2009, p. 5).

What is the problem? Phelan (2014, p. 38) argues this is a "negative … freedom", freedom "is defined primarily as freedom from coercion, especially the coercive actions of the state". Help could be coercion; if I help you, you will not help yourself. Individual responsibility leads to help becoming transactional: an individual choosing to engage with a provider as a way of 'helping themselves'. The citizen is a worker, working for themselves, the "autonomous man" ideally "self-sufficient, self-reliant, self-realising" (Grahame & Marston, 2012, p. 76). Read (2009, p. 35) says neoliberalism is "privatisation all the way down". Your beliefs, behaviours, economics, and mental or physical health are yours to deal with, and you will be better for dealing with it.

Neoliberalism makes self-responsibility the panacea to poverty and unemployment. How? Aggressive obligations to push/punish the recipients of welfare to flourish. Suppose you do not take these obligations/opportunities. From this psychological or work effort perspective, sociological or systemic explanations are rejected as just excuses for the poor to do the 'wrong thing' (Wacquant, 2009, pp. 8–11). When we can blame the poor, we are exonerating society and government from helping the poor because it is the poor person's effort that is failing.

Australian welfare follows this trend. Welfare recipients participate with an entirely private employment service to 'assist' them into work (Bennett et al., 2018). Australia, like most liberal welfare states (Esping-Andersen, 1990) constantly imply poverty and unemployment are means of leisure, laziness, and an apathy. As with most ways of talking about the poor they are accentuated, rather than attenuated when trying to avoid the stereotype. For example, the Senate committee's (2004) report on poverty and financial hardship was titled 'A hand up not a hand out' or more recently the *Employment Services 2020* report (2018) titled 'I want to work'. These phrases reflect, by their avoidance, the dominant ideas that welfare recipients are dependents for which employment will solve their problems. The title of the 2020 report title by opposing the dispositional stereotype paradoxically enshrines disposition as the default explanation for poverty and unemployment. The title and recommendations repeatedly encourage "Personal Responsibility" and "Independence" (Employment Services, 2018, pp. 4, 5, 13, 14, 15, 24, 50, 52, 62). But what are these contexts like to live in?

Contexts of Australian Poverty

There were many contexts described in books and articles as essential to understanding poverty in Australia:

- Welfare provision and effects of policy changes, especially for women and single mothers
- Housing and housing policy
- Food choices, an example of 'rational choices'
- The experience of single mothers
- Particular pervasive issues
  - Discourses on welfare
  - The digital divide
  - Education
  - Health
  - Intergenerational effects
  - Human–computer
  - Interactions

All literature involved some reference to policy or policy change. The findings of the texts overlapped constantly, though often the topics and academic fields were diverse, so inter-referencing was limited.

Two Great Australian Books

The two most informative Australian texts were two books. Mark Peel's (2003) *The Lowest Rung*, as Professor of Modern Cultural and Social History, interviewed 300 participants from Inala, Mount Druitt, and Broadmeadows (Queensland). What participants said about their situation resonated from experience, from history, not the past causing their current situations but rather the past as an experience in the present and how remembering affected them (p. 11; see Guerin 2015, 2016). Much of their reported feelings echoed from parts of their lives now missing or gone, such as good jobs, or just 'good times'. Even 'getting by' in the present accompanied sadness for those around them, especially unemployed men (pp. 114–116). Participants were fearful of reoccurring insecurities (p. 123). The systems that treat poor people as untrustworthy, as "bludgers" (pp. 10, 9, 136) and "cheats" (p. 21, 94, 97) as did politicians and media (p. 172) with poor people turning the rhetoric against other poor people (pp. 75–76).

According to Peel, hope for the future relies on listening to the poor: letting the poor determine ways forward and trusting in disadvantaged people. That trust should not be blind trust, but

> [disadvantaged people] are right more often than people would allow ... There is a difference between acknowledging something that works in a particular situation, at a particular time and within particular constraints, and idealising it as the best or only solution.
>
> *(p. 169)*

Luckily, such suggestions for more detail on people's actual lives resonate with changes in the landscape of psychology research such as the Power Threat Meaning Framework (Johnstone & Boyle, 2018), psychology about human beings (Valsiner et al., 2016), reassessments of subjectivity (Højholt & Schraube, 2019), and rethinking psychology as a social science (this series).

John Murphy et al.'s book, *Half a citizen: Life on welfare in Australia*, followed Peel's lead (p. 3). Both books take direct aim at the problematic 'behavioural' explanations of poverty. Murphy et al. (2011) included 150 interviews over three years. Financial constraints, low income, or poverty were the recruitment criteria, but participants spoke of other constraints once interviewed. Some of those issues were:

- Limited suburb affordability, and stigma affecting relationships (p. 18)
- Physical and mental health issues, and their treatments, as deprivation (p. 71)
- Exclusion by unemployment; losing friends from work; unable to socialise (p. 74)
- Five-day work week limits self-determination (pp. 98–99)
- Single parents are full-time carers, limiting working availability (p. 109)
- Strategies to "undermine" control of welfare bureaucracy (p. 150)

These constraints were contrasted by the opportunities to get resources. For example, dumpster-dived food can be healthier than buying cheap food (p. 63). Further participants were not as disconnected as you may think: "The rhetoric of public policy often assumes that welfare recipients are socially disconnected and disengaged from the wider community and need assistance in order to be included, but we found much evidence to support a contrasting view" (pp. 68–69).

Connecting to others included cases of 'using up relationships' with no lasting connection. As an example, their participant 'Mallory' (p. 60) gave sugar to other housing commission block tenants only to end up with no sugar of her own. Mallory could not ask those other tenants for sugar back. When little to no reciprocity is possible relationships suffer. Some were left with no social network, otherwise, employment and workmates may be their only social contact (p. 82). Poverty for these participants was not just what is missing but also how they got things through other people.

That all noted, these books should be read in full to gain the image of poverty they provide.

The Contexts across the Literature

Table 4.1 contains the many themes I found useful for a snapshot of contexts for Australian poverty. A version of this table with full referencing can be found in my thesis (Thain, 2020).

And It All Happens at Once ...

All these things happen together and separating them out makes the reality of poverty disappear. Psychological research easily falls into this hole, despite calls for contextualisation: "Further study with a focus on participant money practices in the context of key relationships would provide greater depth to our understanding of how neoliberal subjectivities are embedded in specific social and relational practices" (Verdouw, 2017, p. 536). Consider just some of interactions described below.

Most participants in my review, unsurprisingly, were in some contact with welfare bureaucracy. These interactions were mostly with Centrelink staff (central government welfare agency), but also the staff of a Job Network Provider (private companies with a government contract). Increasingly there are moves towards an automatic digital system which monitors and allows recipients of welfare to carry out their work-related obligations alone while many poor people are affected by the digital divide – without consistent internet access.

Frontline workers, in a variety of services, could be infantilising and authoritative, and citizens did not know their rights to resist such treatment (McDonald & Marston, 2005; Ulmestig & Marston, 2015; Considine et al., 2003). Such approaches were harmful for participants psychologically and behaviourally (Mason et al., 2014). Resisting frontline workers' suggestion

TABLE 4.1 Shared Contexts in Australian Qualitative Research with 'The Poor'

Theme

Welfare system and bureaucracy

- Paperwork issues
- Issues with professional power (e.g., doctors determining disability)
- Wastes time
- Front line workers authoritative or unhelpful
- Worry about surveillance
- Lack of knowledge of rights and procedures
- Helpful workers are the minority
- Issues from 'Mutual Obligations'
  - People could do things alone but were not allowed
  - Overzealous or unwarranted punishment
  - Expansion to people with disability
  - Negatives from doing what is expected
- System disrespected clients (infantilising and degrading)
- Reductions in payments harmed livelihood

Food

- Missing out was common
- Long justifications for purchases (especially for mothers with children)

Stigma

- Stigma based on place (suburb)
  - People and place are reputationally entangled
- People spoke of not being that 'person' while living in stigmatised places
- Some hide poverty to avoid stigma

Neoliberalism

- Detrimental to participants
  - Some poor people explicitly agreed with neoliberal ideals
    - E.g., For *some poor people* it is their own fault for not trying
- Some agreement that they need to get better at money behaviours
- Emotional strain of feeling personally responsible for poverty
- Ways of challenging neoliberalism were limited but present (Verdouw, 2017)

Psychological effects

- Anxiety from poverty
  - Many stressful life events
  - Embarrassment and shame with and because of others
- Depression from poverty
  - Self-worth issues from comparison to others (blamed self)
- Trauma from poverty or led to poverty

Housing

- High costs (rent and mortgage)
- Long waits for public housing
- Unemployment impeding rental housing success
- Lack of security
- Interpersonal issues – roommates, family, 'others'

(*Continued*)

TABLE 4.1 (Continued)

Theme

Internalisation
- Blaming the self
- Accepted the 'give and take' (agreed with mutual obligations being needed)

Employment
- Agreement work is central to good living
- Harmful jobs and the need for better jobs
- Discrimination (on age, gender, race, and health)
- Low availability of both high skill and low skill work
- Digital skills and access for job search and job performance needed
- History of unemployment reduces opportunities (e.g., getting rental approval)
- Need for more qualifications and overqualification

Digital divide
- Lack of technology or access – harmed job searching
- Lack of skill – harmed employability
- Led to an information divide (limited health info, education, knowledge in general)

Health
- Lack of affordability for care and insurance
- Access
  - Ill health leading to lost resources (missing out on work)
- Worsened interpersonal issues (reliant on others as carers)
- Nutrition a key concern (esp. mothers)
- Healthy homes (lack of heating, cooling, or structural issues lead to health complaints)

Financial
- Lack of money problematic (often welfare inadequacy)
- Rent and bills come first (food second, social life and specialised problems last)
- Single parents (mothers) are not supported financially (esp. limited child support)
- The focus on money over people can be a problem in itself
- Counteractive strategies
  - Buying behaviour creating poverty
  - Saving behaviour creating deprivation

Space/location
- Stigma affected people and places (suburbs)
- Limit by distance from social network or surrounded by new people
- Effects on mental health
- Linked to children's education

Social context
- Network use important for livelihood
  - Lack of support (network is poor too)
  - Took from the network with reciprocation (including charities)
  - Loss of key network or partner could lead to poverty
  - Need for formal assistance for financial goods (welfare with deprivation)
  - Avoidance of some connections (e.g., burdensome family and friends)

TABLE 4.1 (Continued)

Theme
• Civil engagement limited but present • Networking common via digital connection (see digital divide)   • May improve mental health through improving social and cultural capital • Food is part of social life
Cultural context • As part of disadvantage • Food is part of culture • Pervasive lack of respect (humiliation/shame)
Children • Missing out on typical experiences or resources • Parent role as critical (either devalued by others) • Gendered parenting roles (mostly single mothers) • Food goes to children first – mothers go hungry • Education as a primary concern • Reproduce neoliberal narratives and discourses   • Parents are responsible for education and employment to avoid poverty
Research suggestions • Focus more on the personal and individual: goals, assessment, training, experience • Increase acknowledgement of structural elements over individual behavioural factors • Need for context in policy • Need for better images and discourses of 'the poor' • Need for happiness to be a focus • Improve well-being via social improvement • Increase needed in basic resources (including money) • More knowledge on rights needed • Empowerment of the poor in welfare and other institutions (e.g., university)

to do a resume writing course, job search in the office, undertake further training, or accept an unsuitable job deemed suitable can be grounds for breaching (loss of payment).

What surprised me was that frontline workers sometimes scoffed at educational opportunities that participants wanted to pursue (Mason et al., 2014; Saunders et al., 2006). Disability support recipients particularly had frontline workers suggesting that wanting to participate in education decreased the legitimacy of the recipients' disability (Humpage, 2007). So, low education is commonly blamed for the poor's positions but at the same time education can be deterred (Palmer et al., 2004; Saunders et al. 2006, p. 29). Entrance to higher education is already difficult for people of poorer backgrounds due to the cultural and social capital gap between students, which appears as dispositional claims about poor people's attitudes to education (Mallman, 2017). These education and welfare bureaucracy issues further intersected and were worsened by a lack or loss of internet connection or digital skills (Broadbent & Papadopoulos, 2013).

Overall, the welfare bureaucracy is a complicated, and a complicating context for poor Australians who rely on welfare to get by. Despite education seeming to be an, or the, avenue towards prosperity it seems this system and these relationships dissuade poorer people, despite the already high prohibitive factors. The pressure is in favour of employment even if it is short term, low quality, or low pay.

Today more obligations and expectations are placed on single parents. Policies announced while I was collecting data included the ParentingNEXT programme as well as increased surveillance of partnership status – disproportionately effecting young women's freedom, especially sexually. These new policies are also new contexts to explore for possible, and likely, negative mental health complications and changes to social relationships and their connected resources.

Care work for children limited working opportunities. In policy and practice, the role of parenting is continually diminished, and costs of childcare increased to make employment and parenting opposing and competing roles (Barth & Gridley, 2008). Problematic transitions litter the journey of parenting, for example, moving from a Parenting Payment to unemployment benefits have severe implications like loss of income while working more, making parenting harder. Utilities and housing costs are essential to be paid first, then transport, social, and family activities were luxuries to be negotiated, and health care like healthy food or medicine and seeing a specialist, as well as social activities with high costs, were forfeit (McKenzie et al., 2016). All these things worsened through the Covid and post-Covid economic downturns.

In several cases, social relationships, whether with friends, family, or strangers, were suggested to be more harmful than helpful to those in poverty, either directly or due to conflicting expectations. For example, food insecurity may be possible to solve by connecting with family, but the back-and-forth exchanges expected in these social relationships can be burdensome and sometimes are best avoided (Crawford et al., 2014, p. 75). In other situations, family solutions may seem obvious, like parents requesting family members to care for children to allow work. While possible, a mother not caring for her children, and relying on others to do so, carries stigma and judgements (Barth & Gridley, 2008, p. 42). The issues for young men when still raising a family while unable to fulfil the identity of a 'breadwinning man' hint at complications for identity, mental health, and social relationships (Peel, 2003; cf. Fleming, 1997).

Food choice has long been an example of 'correct–incorrect' or 'rational–irrational' choices that poor people 'fail'; choosing healthy food is correct, rational, deliberate, whereas choosing satisfying but unhealthy food is incorrect, irrational, intuitive. Single parents, or rather single mothers – historically most criticised for their choices – are the focus. Unsurprisingly having no money makes choices difficult but there was a specific goal: the well-being of their children (Barth & Gridley, 2008). Satiation, in particular, directed food selection, avoiding a child complaining to others that they were hungry. Still parents needed to display complex rationalisations for buying including balancing against costs, healthy versus unhealthy, and perishability (Burns et al., 2013; McKenzie et al., 2016). The reputational damage possible from a hungry child versus buying small amounts of healthier food is not a simple dichotomy of correct–incorrect.

Poverty gets complicated when losing social relationships and exchanges. The mothers that were struggling grappled with frontline workers who did not understand the issues of mothering and fathers who did not pay support payments (Natalier et al., 2016). A breakdown of or death in relationships can lead to losses in material stability, such as losing accommodation (Morris, 2013, p. 50). In some cases, the breakdown of these relationships can be a good thing, even when it brings poverty, for example the many women escaping abusive relationships. In other cases, material instability only compounds the pain from relationship loss. So, losing a relationship is not simply good or bad, but highly contextual. This is before we even consider the more esoteric effects on identity that social and cultural capital have (Mallman, 2014).

The idea that more relationships and resources are good is wrong. Social inclusion and exclusion are useful starting points, but complexity in relationships is much more impactful. Social inclusion is not a blanket solution to individual problems, even if individual's inclusion in civic and economic life benefits society. The examples above are still broken up more than they should be. More interconnections, intersections, and entanglements are possible. And I and others know we should not separate out poverty experiences from contexts:

> It is the deep embeddedness of the production of subjectivity in the social and cultural that we are exploring here. The social-cultural and psychological are so strongly entwined with each other that a disciplinary teasing apart does violence to their actual mechanisms.
>
> *(Walkerdine et al., 2001, p. 15)*

Research in Other Western Democracies

There is some transferability between Australia and other liberal welfare states (the United States, UK, NZ; as per Esping-Andersen, 1990). A few books require special mention: Matthew Desmond's *Evicted: Poverty and profit in the*

American city (2016), also see Desmond's more recent *Poverty: By America* (2023) and Joan Maya Mazelis's *Surviving poverty: Creating sustainable ties among the poor* (2017). As it was with the previous Australian books, it is not entirely helpful to break the deep data and arguments down to a paragraph of a few pithy points, rather these texts should be read in full for their unique and important perspective of poverty. The findings of some of these books are incorporated into the topics below through journal articles which drew on the same data (Desmond, 2012a, 2012b; Mazelis, 2015).

Summary of Topics and Methods – Differences to Australian Research

The disciplines that investigated poverty were much more diverse internationally than compared to Australia, maybe just due to sheer quantity: there are more researchers to consider. Of interest is that anthropology and geography featured more in the international sample exploring urban, or metropolitan poverty than in the Australian literature. Sociology and social policy were again the most common. Also, psychology provided minimal input in Australian literature (4, 6.8%), while psychology-trained researchers accounted for 13.6% of international first authors but in sociology and social policy journals.

The topics covered were much more diverse than the Australian literature. The Australian literature was mostly focused on the welfare system with some health and economic considerations, while many of the international literature examined much more specific issues. The sample covered a large range of issues, including general investigations of poverty and exclusion, family-specific investigations, health determinates, mental health-related experiences, transitions to adulthood, and many gender-related texts. Housing and food appeared again as key resources and monetary choices were analysed, particularly food choices.

Contexts from International Research

Dispositional Stigma from Strangers

Finding the cause of poverty inside people was directly challenged. Studies found complex strategies to meet needs (Barnes, 2008; Dagdeviren et al., 2017; Roy et al., 2004). Several texts reported avoidance of being identified as poor by dressing in certain ways that mitigate 'looking poor' (Langille-Hoppe et al., 2010, pp. 130–131), or ways to limit monitoring by welfare systems (Cook, 2012, p. 523). The effects of stigma seemed similar across nations, especially others 'looking down' on the poor (Underlid, 2005). Again, some participants did not recognise or rejected their own poverty (Garthwaite, 2014, pp. 792–793; Milbourne, 2014; Shildrick & MacDonald, 2013).

Social Relationships and Identity

Several texts directly addressed social relationships. Desmond (2012a) explained the strategies around relationships of the urban poor and the use of 'disposable ties'. Participants were able to build up relationships to gain what is needed, but due to a lack of resources or an inability to maintain the relationship, a sudden 'disposal' of that social connection occurred. Other literature also examined how trust within social networks is needed for single mothers' strategies (Burton et al., 2009; Freeman & Dodson, 2014). Identity formation for college students was also tied to their relationships through their social class background (Aries & Seider, 2007). The loss of relationships by poverty or other issues reoccurred as well (St. Vil et al., 2017).

Welfare Bureaucracy

While the literature covered a variety of different policies the research resulted in startlingly similar responses from participants. Onerous monitoring of welfare systems led to feeling powerless, disrespected, and uncared for by frontline workers (Ali et al., 2018, pp. 2794–2798; Altman & Goldberg, 2008, p. 78; Underlid, 2005, p. 277). Representations of the poor, the sick, the disabled, and welfare recipients in the media and by politicians found this same disrespect replicated in everyday life by strangers (Garthwaite, 2014, p. 189). Welfare conditionality, particularly in the UK, echoed many of the findings from Australian studies due to the remarkably similar policy decisions that have occurred (see Dean, 2007; Patrick, 2011, 2014; Shefer et al., 2016). Bureaucratic and interpersonal issues were found in the experiences of low-income people's health care as in Australia (Becker & Newsom, 2003; Sieppert et al., 2004).

Mental Health

Shefer et al. (2016) was one of the few qualitative studies looking at mental health and having some psychological input. The punitive welfare systems, which removed payments from those with mental health issues, increased the mental illness symptoms which, often, had originally produced unemployment (p. 840). Other cases of considering mental health and poverty found that welfare support was lacking, and many went without necessities or needed to borrow from family or strangers while also losing social relationships due to their poverty (Wilton, 2003). Most literature contained cases in which frontline workers or policy decisions had directly anxiety-producing effects (the United States: Altman & Goldberg, 2008; UK: Garthwaite, 2014, pp. 791–792). Otherwise, exclusion in the form of being out of work was reported to harm mental health and self-esteem (Cushon et al., 2010; Stewart et al., 2008). Anxiety also came about from a lack of knowledge on rights and the welfare system (the United States: Altman & Goldberg, 2008, p. 87; Australia and Sweden: Ulmestig & Marston, 2015).

Housing and Accommodation

Literature collected on housing examined the experience in more depth than the Australian texts. Desmond's *Eviction* study (2012b), for example, was particularly detailed, using both statistical and ethnographic work to find that the mechanisms of eviction served to directly reproduce urban poverty. Other studies were able to tie participants' histories, including early parental loss, health issues, mortality implications, social networks, labour inequalities and sexuality, all through the lens of poverty and homelessness (Berman et al., 2015). These findings also highlighted the importance of social relationships, or rather their absence or loss, as a key determining factor in losing resources and then entering or maintaining poverty. One psychiatric paper found help in social relationships could change this outcome for excluded participants (Sheridan et al., 2018).

Food Insecurity

The international literature revealed more of the complexity of an often-simplified basic resource: food. The meaning behind shopping at high-quality stores and buying high-quality food items challenge the simplification of what people consider "worth it" being about cost and health (Tach & Amorim, 2015, pp. 825–827). The symbolic and cultural values of food emphasised the issues inherent in constructing a model of 'a good life', and challenge the focus on quantity over quality. Structural factors, such as place, time, transport, income flows, were common blocks to getting healthy and "better" food opposing the assumption that poor people lack the knowledge or will to eat healthy (Tach & Amorim, 2015; Zachary et al., 2013). Participants in the international and Australian samples further relied on food they could acquire through charities, social relationships, dumpster diving, and food banks.

Low-income earners either in welfare receipt, or insecure, or poorly paid employment, often had health issues exacerbated by the poor quality of food they had available while being fully aware they should be eating a healthier diet (Garthwaite et al., 2015; Garthwaite, 2016; Sieppert et al., 2004). Stigma and embarrassment was common when using food banks. Stigma was linked to harmful representations of the poor in 'poverty porn' on television: a genre of shows which display poor people and their struggles for entertainment often reinforcing the lazy and violent tropes in "a practice of othering" (Garthwaite, 2016, p. 284). The experience of dumpster diving was also investigated, revealing a variety of reasons to access food in such a stigmatised way (Vinegar et al., 2016). Dumpster diving requires specialised knowledge making this a difficult pathway for food. Further, dumpster divers who were food insecure were also socially isolated, while some richer divers were well-connected and otherwise food-secure.

Women and Mothers

The expectations on women, and what it means to be a woman is more complicated than ever. As women move into adulthood, they are expected to take on care work of children and men as mothers, but also become self-sufficient workers as neoliberal subjects (Broughton, 2003; Broussard et al., 2012; Dodson & Dickert, 2004; Gazso, 2007; Hicks, 2005; Pulkingham et al., 2010; Marsh-McDonald & Schroeder, 2012; Strother, 2004; St. Vil et al., 2017; Woodward, 2008). The judgement and expectation of family, friends, and strangers were constant. These types of expectations bleed over to how parents treat their economics, primarily as topics that are taboo to engage in conversations about, even with their own children (Romo, 2011). Economic and financial expectations of parents, especially mothers, help to place an identity on them as the centre of wrongdoing and failure. Losing or escaping of problematic relationships again appeared as a starting point for poverty.

Over a third of international literature exclusively examined the experiences of women, some explicitly focused on mothers. Some texts considered a lack of masculine perspectives as a limitation of their findings (Ali et al., 2018, p. 2802; Cook, 2012). One possible reason for the lack of research found with men who are in poverty may be that men are often taught to avoid speaking openly on sensitive topics which qualitative research requires. Otherwise, the issue may be that search strategies linking poverty and masculine experiences more about seeing as men and masculine first, and as poor, excluded, or deprived second. If that is the case, data on men's poverty would not appear without specific masculine terms. The lack of data from men is problematic but I want to report what I found as a student searching not a perfect search. Regardless, we now have a huge array of contexts that we can expect to find in poverty, but we still have the question: what is poverty?

What Is Poverty in Qualitative Literature?

Surprisingly, searching for this answer in this literature garnered very little. The few times poverty definitions were directly addressed provided a clear but uncritical answer. For example, "Ours was a qualitative study, and we were most interested in interviewees' accounts and definitions of poverty. **These were usually very much at odds with objective measures**" (Shildrick & MacDonald, 2013, p. 288, emphasis added). Poverty is an active constant process for participants, and often defining yourself as poor can be shameful, so many participants spoke about themselves as 'managing' or 'not that poor'.

Still there is a juxtaposition of material personal poverty, when interviewees could not feed and clothe themselves, while denying that you are poor because you are 'getting by'.

Other studies provided more nuanced and creative perspectives on what poverty is. For a Canadian poor women's group, social relationships were a central element of a good life, and loss of relationships was central to their poverty (Collins, 2005). Material goods were important, but money was only indirectly mentioned to get those material goods. Feelings of stress, fear, isolation, guilt, being continually monitored, and having debt marked their low-income status, but again these women said they were not part of the other destitute group (pp. 18–21).

Otherwise, women in the United States defined their success and poverty as, again, dependent on other people and their relationships. Some US participants viewed poverty as persecution, by the punitive surveillance-based welfare system, and as a mindset of hopelessness (Marsh-McDonald & Schroeder, 2012). In other cases, the very creation of definitions of poverty by professionals are at odds with the definitions by the poor themselves, the former "securing dominance within the culture by implying that those who do not conform are abnormal" (Langille-Hoppe et al., 2010, p. 126).

I included one study that ran into the definitions issue seeming without intending it. Snow et al. (2017) investigated "sharing saving and living well on less" as part of human–computer interaction. By the end of the research, they concluded that the 'low-income' recruitment criterion was "wrongly assumed" as a good starting point (p. 353). Low-income as a focus is reductive. The findings showed that time-based elements such as job acquisition and loss, as well as interactions between mental illness and employment, which impacted stability, were powerful controlling elements in their participants' lives. Further, that overcoming these issues happened through other people. Snow, Vyas, and Brereton suggest a new concept to replace 'low income' called "Social-Financial Connectedness" (p. 354) which includes how resources, like money, function with and for family and friends. The idea, while not fully formed, was included to provoke challenges to the assumption of 'low-income' as a focus and its suitability in further studies. On the other hand, throughout most qualitative literature, the issue of defining poverty, from the perspective of the poor, is either avoided, or seen as an issue too complicated for research.

Stress and Stressful Life Events

Psychology's 'cognitive feedback loop' for poverty includes stress as the instigating 'factor' for the loop. One clear finding above is that 'stressful events' are social. Relationship breakdowns may seem like obvious stressor but through this literature I saw the powerful effects of constant, forced, stranger relationships through governmental and organisational bureaucracies. Otherwise, the issue of isolation in poverty prevailed, "I just learnt to deal with what I'm feeling and keep it in there ... not knowing who to speak to, but it would be nice to just let it out ... how I'm feeling" (Participant in Barth & Gridley, 2008, p. 41).

There is a high degree of complexity in relationships. Some women spoke of wanting a new male partner as a "white knight" providing salvation from homelessness and poverty (Sharam, 2017, p. 54), while at the opposite end some single mothers, as an overrepresented group in poverty, had desperately escaped abusive relationships which generated their poverty (Natalier et al., 2016). In other cases, such as Murphy et al. (2011), the exclusion of the poor was questioned. The absence of helpful social relationships, as well as their burden or assistance, complicates exploring relational poverty.

Welfare provision is a particularly powerful stressor. The very efforts to combat low income and poverty may be functioning to keep people poor and unemployed, and a major contributor of stress in the feedback loop. 'Life-first' and place-based employment programmes aimed at helping with problems other than unemployment were argued for and found to be more helpful than the traditional punitive systems (Dean, 2003, 2009; Mason et al., 2014, p. 649; Walker et al., 2016, p. 518).

In many cases, making a 'correct' choice was extremely confusing. For example, some participants worried about losing welfare income support by going over the thresholds due to temporary employment which seemed to result in losing money (Arthurson & Jacobs, 2009, pp. 186–187; Peel, 2003, p. 124). Assessments or reassessments of eligibility, such as disability assessment, could result in a loss of welfare benefits (Garthwaite, 2014). Choosing to take employment opportunities for money can result in being considered a 'bad mother' (Underlid, 2005, p. 278; Dodson, 2013, p. 273). Sometimes participants were anxious or stressed about the future (McKenzie et al., 2016, p. 6), about loss of rental tenure (Morris et al., 2017), about relationship loss (Burton et al., 2009; Sharam, 2017), or issues of insecurity (Mallman, 2017, p. 2044). In most, if not all, situation the wrong choice was the one that created judgements of being unworthy for support made by others around the poor.

Conclusion

The contexts of poverty include many other people, systems, and processes as part of the choices, issues, and constraints that poor people are battling with constantly. An important final note in this chapter is that this is just ultimately a list. There is more detail in every person's life, and each case of poverty will present another real person's story with this list of possible contexts coming together to affect that person in a unique way. This is our jumping off point.

From the general societal to the individual contextualised cases, remember what you have learned so far, and start to see poverty contextually when you observe it in everyday life.

References

Ali, S., Sensoy Bahar, O., Gopalan, P., Lukasiewicz, K., Parker, G., McKay, M., & Walker, R. (2018). "Feeling less than a second class citizen": Examining the emotional consequences of poverty in New York City. *Journal of Family Issues, 39*(10), 2781–2805. https://doi.org/10.1177/0192513X18760348

Altman, J. C., & Goldberg, G. S. (2008). The quality of life paradox: A study of former public assistance recipients. *Journal of Poverty, 11*(4), 71–90. doi:10.1300/J134v11n04_04

Aries, E., & Seider, M. (2007). The role of social class in the formation of identity: A study of public and elite private college students. *The Journal of Social Psychology, 147*(2), 137–157. https://doi.org/10.3200/SOCP.147.2.137-157

Arthurson, K., & Jacobs, K. (2009). Discourses about Australian social housing, social exclusion and employment: Indications of the post-welfare state?. *Housing, Theory and Society, 26*(3), 179–192. doi:10.1080/14036090801939828

Barnes, S. L. (2008). A case study of the working poor single mother experience: An analysis of the structure versus agency discourse. *Journal of Poverty, 12*(2), 175–200. doi:10.1080/10875540801973575

Barth, M., & Gridley, H. (2008). Families living in poverty in Broadmeadows: Challenges, survival strategies and support services. *Australian Community Psychologist, 20*(1), 36–46.

Becker, G., & Newsom, E. (2003). Socioeconomic status and dissatisfaction with health care among chronically ill African Americans. *American Journal of Public Health, 93*(5), 742–748. https://doi.org/10.2105/ajph.93.5.742

Bennett, O., Dawson, E., Lewis, A., O'Halloran, D., & Smith, W. (2018). *Working it out: Employment services in Australia*. Percapita & Australian Unemployed Workers Union. September 2018. Retrieved from: https://percapita.org.au/wp-content/uploads/2018/09/Working-It-Out-FINAL.pdf

Berman, L. R., Snow, R. C., Moorman, J. D., Policicchio, D., Geronimus, A. T., & Padilla, M. B. (2015). Parental loss and residential instability: The impact on young women from low-income households in Detroit. *Journal of Child and Family Studies, 24*(2), 416–426. doi:10.1007/s10826-013-9852-9

Broadbent, R., & Papadopoulos, T. (2013). Bridging the digital divide – An Australian story. *Behaviour & Information Technology, 32*(1), 4–13. http://dx.doi.org/10.1080/0144929X.2011.572186

Broughton, C. (2003). Reforming poor women: The cultural politics and practices of welfare reform. *Qualitative Sociology, 26*(1), 35–51. https://doi.org/10.1023/A:1021451903511

Broussard, C. A., Joseph, A. L., & Thompson, M. (2012). Stressors and coping strategies used by single mothers living in poverty. *Affilia, 27*(2), 190–204. doi:10.1177/0886109912443884

Burns, C., Cook, K., & Mavoa, H. (2013). Role of expendable income and price in food choice by low income families. *Appetite, 71*, 209–217. http://dx.doi.org/10.1016/j.appet.2013.08.018

Burton, L. M., Cherlin, A., Winn, D. M., Estacion, A., & Holder-Taylor, C. (2009). The role of trust in low-income mothers' intimate unions. *Journal of Marriage and Family, 71*(5), 1107–1124. https://doi.org/10.1111/j.1741-3737.2009.00658.x

Carr, S. C. (2013). *Anti-poverty psychology*. Springer Science & Business Media.

Collins, S. B. (2005). An understanding of poverty from those who are poor. *Action Research, 3*(1), 9–31. doi:10.1177/1476750305047983

Connell, R. (2010). Understanding neoliberalism. In S. Braedley & M. Luxton (eds.), *Neoliberalism and everyday life* (pp. 22–36). McGill-Queen's University Press.

Considine, M., Ziguras, S., & Dufty, G. (2003). *Much obliged: Disadvantaged job seekers' experiences of the mutual obligation regime.* Brotherhood of Saint Laurence, St Vincent de Paul Society & The Centre for Public Policy. Available from http://library.bsl.org.au/jspui/bitstream/1/6152/1/Much_obliged_final.pdf

Cook, K. (2012). Neoliberalism, welfare policy and health: A qualitative meta-synthesis of single parents' experience of the transition from welfare to work. *Health, 16*(5), 507–530. doi:10.1177/1363459311434650

Crawford, B., Yamazaki, R., Franke, E., Amanatidis, S., Ravulo, J., Steinbeck, K., … & Torvaldsen, S. (2014). Sustaining dignity? Food insecurity in homeless young people in urban Australia. *Health Promotion Journal of Australia, 25*(2), 71–78. http://dx.doi.org/10.1071/HE13090

Cushon, J. A., Muhajarine, N., & Labonte, R. (2010). Lived experience of economic and political trends related to globalization. *Canadian Journal of Public Health, 101*(1), 92–95. doi:10.1007/BF03405571. PMID: 20364547; PMCID: PMC6974066.

Dagdeviren, H., Donoghue, M., & Meier, L. (2017). The narratives of hardship: The new and the old poor in the aftermath of the 2008 crisis in Europe. *The Sociological Review, 65*(2), 369–385. https://doi.org/10.1111/1467-954X.12403

Dean, H. (2003). Discursive repertoires and the negotiation of well-being: Reflections on the WeD frameworks. ESRC Research Group on *Wellbeing in developing countries Working Paper 4*. Available from http://citeseerx.ist.psu.edu/viewdoc/download?doi=10.1.1.476.2945&rep=reTeresa&type=pdf

Dean, H. (2007). The ethics of welfare-to-work. *Policy & Politics, 35*(4), 573–589. doi:https://doi.org/10.1332/030557307782453029

Dean, H. (2009). Critiquing capabilities: The distractions of a beguiling concept. *Critical Social Policy, 29*(2), 261–278. doi:10.1177/0261018308101629

Desmond, M. (2012a). Disposable ties and the urban poor. *American Journal of Sociology, 117*(5), 1295–1335. https://doi.org/10.1086/663574

Desmond, M. (2012b). Eviction and the reproduction of urban poverty. *American Journal of Sociology, 118*(1), 88–133. https://doi.org/10.1086/666082

Desmond, M. (2016). *Evicted: Poverty and profit in the American city*. Broadway Books.

Dodson, L. (2013). Stereotyping low-wage mothers who have work and family conflicts. *Journal of Social Issues, 69*(2), 257–278. https://doi.org/10.1111/josi.12014

Dodson, L., & Dickert, J. (2004). Girls' family labor in low-income households: A decade of qualitative research. *Journal of Marriage and Family, 66*(2), 318–332. https://doi.org/10.1111/j.1741-3737.2004.00023.x

Employment Services. (2018). *I want to work, Employment Services 2020 Report*. Commonwealth of Australia.

Esping-Andersen, G. (1990). *Three worlds of welfare capitalism*. Princeton University Press.

Fleming, R. (1997). *The common purse: Income sharing in New Zealand families.* Auckland University Press.
Freeman, A. L., & Dodson, L. (2014). Social network development among low-income single mothers: Potential for bridging, bonding, and building. *Family Relations, 63*(5), 589–601. https://doi.org/10.1111/fare.12088
Garthwaite, K. (2014). Fear of the brown envelope: Exploring welfare reform with long-term sickness benefits recipients. *Social Policy & Administration, 48*(7), 782–798. doi:10.1111/spol.12049
Garthwaite, K. (2016). Stigma, shame and 'people like us': An ethnographic study of foodbank use in the UK. *Journal of Poverty and Social Justice, 24*(3), 277–289. http://dx.doi.org/10.1332/175982716X14721954314922
Garthwaite, K. A., Collins, P. J., & Bambra, C. (2015). Food for thought: An ethnographic study of negotiating ill health and food insecurity in a UK foodbank. *Social Science & Medicine, 132*, 38–44. http://dx.doi.org/10.1016/j.socscimed.2015.03.019
Gazso, A. (2007). Balancing expectations for employability and family responsibilities while on social assistance: Low-income mothers' experiences in three Canadian provinces. *Family Relations, 56*(5), 454–466. www.jstor.org/stable/4541688
Grahame, T., & Marston, G. (2012). Welfare-to-work policies and the experience of employed single mothers on income support in Australia: Where are the benefits?. *Australian Social Work, 65*(1), 73–86. http://dx.doi.org/10.1080/0312407X.2011.604093
Guerin, B. (2015). *How to rethink psychology: New metaphors for understanding people and their behavior*. Routledge.
Guerin, B. (2016). *How to rethink human behavior: A practical guide to social contextual analysis*. Routledge.
Hicks, D. (2005). Class readings: Story and discourse among girls in working-poor America. *Anthropology & Education Quarterly, 36*(3), 212–229.
Højholt, C., & Schraube E. (2019) *Subjectivity and knowledge*. Springer.
Humpage, L. (2007). Models of disability, work and welfare in Australia. *Social Policy & Administration, 41*(3), 215–231. https://doi.org/10.1111/j.1467-9515.2007.00549.x
Johnstone, L., & Boyle, M. with Cromby, J., Dillon, J., Harper, D., Kinderman, P., Longden, E., Pilgrim, D., & Read, J. (2018). *The Power Threat Meaning Framework: Towards the identification of patterns in emotional distress, unusual experiences and troubled or troubling behaviour, as an alternative to functional psychiatric diagnosis.* British Psychological Society.
Langille-Hoppe, M. M., Gonzalez, J. R., Maxey, M., & Terrell, S. (2010). "What makes you think I'm poor?" A qualitative analysis of etic and emic perceptions of poverty in the Ozarks. *Journal of Ethnographic & Qualitative Research, 4*(3), 125–138
Lister, R. (2004). *Poverty*. Polity Press.
Mallman, M. (2017). The perceived inherent vice of working-class university students. *The Sociological Review, 65*(2), 235–250doi:10.1111/1467-954X.12422
Marsh-McDonald, C. M., & Schroeder, S. (2012). Women in transition: A qualitative analysis of definitions of poverty and success. *Qualitative Report, 17*, 91.
Mason, C., Spinks, A., Hajkowicz, S., & Hobman, L. (2014). Exploring the contribution of frontline welfare service delivery to capability development in Australia. *Journal of Social Policy, 43*(3), 635–653.

Mazelis, J. M. (2015). "I got to try to give back": How reciprocity norms in a poor people's organization influence members' social capital. *Journal of Poverty, 19*(1), 109–131. https://doi.org/10.1080/10875549.2014.979458

Mazelis, J. M. (2017). *Surviving poverty: Creating sustainable ties among the poor*. NYU Press.

McDonald, C., & Marston, G. (2005). Workfare as welfare: Governing unemployment in the advanced liberal state. *Critical Social Policy, 25*(3), 374–401. doi:10.1177/0261018305054077

McKenzie, H. J., McHugh, C., & McKay, F. H. (2016). Life on newstart allowance: A new reality for low-income single mothers. *Journal of Family Studies, 25*(1), 18–33. doi:10.1080/13229400.2016.1200114

Milbourne, P. (2014). Poverty, place, and rurality: Material and sociocultural disconnections. *Environment and Planning A, 46*(3), 566–580.

Morris, A. (2013). The trajectory towards marginality: How do older Australians find themselves dependent on the private rental market?. *Social Policy and Society, 12*(1), 47–59. doi:10.1017/S1474746412000383

Morris, A., Hulse, K., & Pawson, H. (2017). Long-term private renters: Perceptions of security and insecurity. *Journal of Sociology, 53*(3), 653–669. doi:10.1177/1440783317707833

Murphy, J., Murray, S., Chalmers, J., Martin, S., & Marston, G. (2011). *Half a citizen: Life on welfare in Australia*. Allen & Unwin.

Natalier, K., Cook, K., & Pitman, T. (2016). Payee mothers' interactions with the department of human services-child support. *Family Matters*, 97, 30.

Palmer, C., Ziersch, A., Arthurson, K., & Baum, F. (2004). Challenging the stigma of public housing: Preliminary findings from a qualitative study in South Australia. *Urban Policy and Research, 22*(4), 411–426. doi:10.1080/0811114042000296326

Patrick, R. (2011). Disabling or enabling: The extension of work-related conditionality to disabled people. *Social Policy and Society, 10*(3), 309–320. doi:10.1017/S1474746411000042

Patrick, R. (2014). Working on welfare: Findings from a qualitative longitudinal study into the lived experiences of welfare reform in the UK. *Journal of Social Policy, 43*(4), 705–725. doi:10.1017/S0047279414000294

Peel, M. (2003). *The lowest rung: Voices of Australian poverty*. Cambridge University Press.

Pemberton, S., Fahmy, E., Sutton, E., & Bell, K. (2016). Navigating the stigmatised identities of poverty in austere times: Resisting and responding to narratives of personal failure. *Critical Social Policy, 36*(1), 21–37. doi:10.1177/0261018315601799

Phelan, S. (2014). *Neoliberalism, media and the political*. Springer.

Pulkingham, J., Fuller, S., & Kershaw, P. (2010). Lone motherhood, welfare reform and active citizen subjectivity. *Critical Social Policy, 30*(2), 267–291. https://doi.org/10.1177/0261018309358292

Read, J. (2009). A genealogy of homo-economicus: Neoliberalism and the production of subjectivity. *Foucault Studies, 6*, 25–36. doi:10.22439/fs.v0i0.2465

Romo, L. K. (2011). Money talks: Revealing and concealing financial information in families. *Journal of Family Communication, 11*(4), 264–281. doi:10.1080/15267431.2010.544634

Roy, K. M., Tubbs, C. Y., & Burton, L. M. (2004). Don't have no time: Daily rhythms and the organization of time for low-income families. *Family Relations*, *53*(2), 168–178. https://doi.org/10.1111/j.0022-2445.2004.00007.x

Saunders, P., Sutherland, K., Davidson, P., Hampshire, A., King, S., & Taylor, J. (2006). *Experiencing poverty – The voices of low-income Australians: towards new indicators of disadvantage project, Stage 1: Focus group outcomes*. Social Policy Research Centre, University of New South Wales.

Senate Community Affairs References Committee. (2004). *A hand up not a hand out: Renewing the fight against poverty Report on poverty and financial hardship*. Commonwealth of Australia.

Sharam, A. (2017). The voices of midlife women facing housing insecurity in Victoria, Australia. *Social Policy and Society*, *16*(1), 49–63. doi:https://doi.org/10.1017/S1474746415000603

Shefer, G., Henderson, C., Frost-Gaskin, M., & Pacitti, R. (2016). Only making things worse: A qualitative study of the impact of wrongly removing disability benefits from people with mental illness. *Community Mental Health Journal*, *52*(7), 834–841. doi:10.1007/s10597-016-0012-8

Sheridan, A., O'Keeffe, D., Coughlan, B., Frazer, K., Drennan, J., & Kemple, M. (2018). Friendship and money: A qualitative study of service users' experiences of participating in a supported socialisation programme. *The International Journal of Social Psychiatry*, *64*(4), 326–334. https://doi.org/10.1177/0020764018763692

Shildrick, T., & MacDonald, R. (2013). Poverty talk: How people experiencing poverty deny their poverty and why they blame 'the poor'. *The Sociological Review*, *61*(2), 285–303. doi:10.1111/1467-954X.12018

Sieppert, J., Te Linde, J., & Rutherford, G. (2004). Poverty as a determinant of health: Capturing the voices of low-income Calgarians. *Canadian Review of Social Policy*, *53*, 122–139.

Snow, S., Vyas, D., & Brereton, M. (2017). Sharing, saving, and living well on less: Supporting social connectedness to mitigate financial hardship. *International Journal of Human–Computer Interaction*, *33*(5), 345–356. doi:10.1080/10447318.2016.1243846

St. Vil, N. M., Sabri, B., Nwokolo, V., Alexander, K. A., & Campbell, J. C. (2017). A qualitative study of survival strategies used by low-income black women who experience intimate partner violence. *Social Work*, *62*(1), 63–71. doi:10.1093/sw/sww080

Stewart, M., Reutter, L., Makwarimba, E., Veenstra, G., Love, R., & Raphael, D. (2008). Left out: Perspectives on social exclusion and inclusion across income groups. *Health Sociology Review*, *17*(1), 78–94. https://doi.org/10.5172/hesr.451.17.1.78

Strother, P. A. (2004). Exit from poverty: How "Welfare Mothers" achieve economic viability. *Journal of Human Behavior in the Social Environment*, *7*(3–4), 97–119. doi:10.1300/J137v07n03_07

Tach, L., & Amorim, M. (2015). Constrained, convenient, and symbolic consumption: Neighborhood food environments and economic coping strategies among the urban poor. *Journal of Urban Health*, *92*(5), 815–834. doi:10.1007/s11524-015-9984-x

Thain, A. (2020). *Rethinking poverty: A qualitative study of becoming resource and relationship constrained in South Australia*. Unpublished PhD Thesis. University of South Australia. https://hdl.handle.net/11541.2/144892

Ulmestig, R., & Marston, G. (2015). Street-level perceptions of procedural rights for young unemployed people – A comparative study between Sweden and Australia. *Social Policy & Administration, 49*(3), 394–411. doi:10.1111/spol.12085

Underlid, K. (2005). Poverty and experiences of social devaluation: A qualitative interview study of 25 long-standing recipients of social security payments. *Scandinavian Journal of Psychology, 46*(3), 273–283. https://doi.org/10.1111/j.1467-9450.2005.00457.x

Valsiner, J., Marsico, G., Chaudhary, N., Sato, T., & Dazzani, V. (eds.). (2016). *Psychology as the science of human being. The Yokohama manifesto*. Annals of theoretical psychology. Springer.

Verdouw, J. J. (2017). The subject who thinks economically? Comparative money subjectivities in neoliberal context. *Journal of Sociology, 53*(3), 523–540. doi:10.1177/1440783316662717

Vinegar, R., Parker, P., & McCourt, G. (2016). More than a response to food insecurity: Demographics and social networks of urban dumpster divers. *Local Environment, 21*(2), 241–253. doi:10.1080/13549839.2014.943708

Wacquant, L. (2009). *Punishing the poor – The neoliberal government of social insecurity*. Duke University Press.

Walker, R., Brown, L., Moskos, M., Isherwood, L., Osborne, K., Patel, K., & King, D. (2016). 'They really get you motivated': Experiences of a life-first employment programme from the perspective of long-term unemployed Australians. *Journal of Social Policy, 45*(3), 507–526. https://doi.org/10.1017/S0047279416000027

Walkerdine, V., Lucey, H., & Melody, J. (2001). *Growing up girl: Psychosocial explorations of gender and class*. Palgrave Macmillan.

Wilton, R. D. (2003). Poverty and mental health: A qualitative study of residential care facility tenants. *Community Mental Health Journal, 39*(2), 139–156. https://doi.org/10.1023/a:1022662704461

Woodward, K. (2008). The multiple meanings of work for welfare-reliant women. *Qualitative Sociology, 31*(2), 149–168. doi:10.1007/s11133-008-9091-3

Zachary, D. A., Palmer, A. M., Beckham, S. W., & Surkan, P. J. (2013). A framework for understanding grocery purchasing in a low-income urban environment. *Qualitative Health Research, 23*(5), 665–678. doi:10.1177/1049732313479451

5

THE EXPERIENCES OF POVERTY

I want to continue telling you about the experiences of people: contexts and pathways for relationships and resources. A more comprehensive and academic description of methods and analysis can be found in my PhD thesis – as well as comprehensive reviews of methods I could not fit in this book (Thain, 2020).

The Analysis

The analysis was based on this book series' previous entries, namely the 2016 book *How to Rethink Human Behaviour* for its core lessons and concepts drawn from across the social sciences. There are many links between those concepts and this analysis.

Resources

Resources are a vital component of poverty concepts and definitions. In several cases, poverty is given the working definition of not having "command over resources" (Hagenaars & Praag, 1985, p. 139; Haveman, 2001, p. 11919; Long, 2010, p. 163; Townsend, 1979, pp. 8, 389; Zambrano, 2014, p. 856). Resources may be absolute, necessary for sustaining life, or relative, bound to the needs of place or people. Resources are a key concept of contextual analysis and, therefore, are required for going beyond money and material possessions.

Within social contextual analysis, resources are defined as, "... any event or things that a population will do something to obtain" (Guerin, 2016, p. 30).

DOI: 10.4324/9781003453970-5

When paired with poverty indicators, we have targets to observe. Focusing on that observation also avoids tracing these to 'basic needs', 'desires', 'eagerness', 'willingness', 'motivations', or other abstract and unobservable concepts inside poor people. Instead, we observe and participate in real lives and find the experiences in the contexts outside of the poor.

Social Relationships

These are "any and all people who are involved in the same resources" (Guerin, 2016, p. 36). These may be called populations, audiences, or social relationships. Money, for example, has several important audiences: your boss, you work for and pays you; your family at home, spends the money; and those owed money, usually strangers in companies. Populations, on the other hand, are broader, involving anyone connected to the resource. For money, this could be consumers of your work, the government who taxes, and generalised others who rely on you or the work for their livelihood.

In previous poverty research relationships were a core focus. Often these were only easily talkable relationships. Murphy et al. (2011) noted that while poor people were expected to be disconnected or excluded from social life, the results of their study did not follow this expectation. Instead, their participants were connected to others but obtained few resources from those relationships. A cursory reflection on modern capitalist Western life will show we interact most often with strangers: people we will never have to interact with again (Beck, 2000; Granovetter, 1985; Guerin, 2016; Polanyi, 1944/2001; Simmel, 1903/1950, 1908/1950). So, we should examine all the people involved not just those social relationships that are salient or easily remembered and named like family and friends.

Resource-Social Relationship Pathways

Many poverty studies focus only on resource management (Saunders et al. 2006), while at other times, resources are ignored when focusing on social relationships (exclusion). Lost is how social relationships and social exchanges are necessary to get resources. Resources then seem independent of those who provide them. I want to avoid that.

To maintain a relationship, you need to *exchange* resources (Simmel, 1907/1971; Granovetter, 1985, 2005; Zelizer, 1994, 2012). Given enough time and observations, these exchange behaviours can be observed and mapped out (Guerin, 2016, p. 41). Resources are almost entirely gained and distributed through other people, whether the shopkeeper sells you food or you get some from a family member. The two cannot be separated: "Poverty is a product of human social relationships because social relationships determine how people distribute resources" (Lemieux & Pratto, 2003, p. 147). That said, investigating pathways is not entirely unique (see Desmond 2012, 2014, 2016; Hodgetts & Stolte, 2017; Mosse, 2010; Sharam & Hulse, 2014).

The Participants

The beginning of explaining my participants is telling you who they were. I want to provide some demographics and why these were important. That said, be wary of thinking that simple demographics give you a real understanding of a person. Kneejerk preconceived notions about who someone is blinds you to what really happens contextually.

Gender

I purposefully recruited six women and three men. Poverty literature highlights the unavoidable gendered context of poverty while it is not necessarily discriminating on gender. The ratio of the community group, however, was overwhelmingly women.

Age

I only interviewed adults, but at the time 17.3% of Australian children lived in income poverty (ACOSS, 2018). So, I purposefully sampled parents' experiences. Furthermore, as older women are an overrepresented group, I sought the experience of older Australians experiences (ACOSS, 2018). Those on aged pension (generally over 65) were not specifically recruited or present in the community.

Payments

All participants were on some form of social security payment. However, in the research period they sometimes moved to a wage and back, compared to a cross-sectional report of 53.3% of people experiencing poverty relying mainly on social security (ACOSS, 2018, p. 27). The payment types generally fit with the range of national statistics and the group's make-up, except for the lack of pension recipients.

Employment Status

All participants had employment, but many were unemployed at some point. Some engaged in only gig work and considered themselves employed; some engaged in part-time work and were underemployed; some considered themselves unemployed despite gigs. This precarious nature of employment is well articulated by Professor Guy Standing (2011).

Education

Education level separated my sample from the community group. Those I spoke to informally often discussed their lack of tertiary education; many had limited secondary education. The bulk of my participants either were completing or had completed tertiary studies. The stories I collected in formal interviews were from particularly confident people, well-versed in telling their story. Others, some with learning difficulties, worries about speaking, or an inability to communicate confidently, did not participate in formal interviews.

Family

Family status is a generalisation of meaningful family connections. The parents spoken to in this study were women, ~95% of single parents are women (DSS, 2018). Seeking the minority group of single fathers was thought to represent such unique contexts and ways of talking, that it should be explored separately – as such contexts would require their own literature reviews and the like.

Housing

I give a simplistic separation between public housing, private rent, ownership, and living with family. Like employment, there were many transitions. A related variable was *transport*. Most participants, and many community members, lived in outer suburban locations; their opportunities for transport into more service-dense areas and to community events was a common complaint and worry. Transport was broken into private and public use, or a combination.

Health Status

All participants and most group members spoke of health concerns, from everyday healthy eating and weight concerns to intermittent health issues, chronic illnesses, mental health issues, disability, and terminal illnesses. I labelled the common presentation as 'general' meaning health issues were present. Still, these ranged from minor physical issues to severe but startlingly frequent mental health issues (anxiety and depression), which were not emphasised by the participant but were still present. All participants reported and spoke about some mental health issues or diagnosed mental health disorders.

Community Participation

I give a time and a quality. Time is split between *intermittent*, meaning the participant sometimes or rarely attended events, and *constant*, meaning they were almost always present. Quality is broken between *extensive*, meaning they participated in various activities with the group, and *limited*, meaning they attended without much participation. Those who disconnected from community group (intermittent, limited) were not actively pursued for more than two interviews. That disconnection also represents the churning nature of group membership.

Background

Table 5.1 does not comment on the cultural, ethnic, or racial background of participants. All participants were white, first-language English, Australian-born, and of European heritage. The group population reflected this too. Other communities and activist groups were present including refugee and Aboriginal and Torres Strait Islander peoples. While strong relationships were present, choices were made in the research design aligned to the ethical and practical needs of the study that limited a wider sampling with these other groups. For this reason, I do not expect these results to represent the experience of anyone outside this given background, just as I do not generalise these results to rural experiences given the metropolitan focus.

Transferability and Trustworthiness

Given these demographics, the experiences explored cannot represent a generalised Australian experience of poverty. Further, participants were well-spoken, educated to tertiary levels, aware of community and political issues, and fighting for change. Experiences of others will vary wildly, as expected in qualitative research (Small, 2009). The experiences explored are personal and individual. I do not claim that this is how poverty is for everyone but rather how poverty can be for someone.

On the other hand, participatory methods and interviews allowed participants to speak not only of their own experiences but also about friends, family, and strangers. Participants spoke about poverty as an experience of their community, explaining differences and similarities between those who understood and those who did not. All participants included their families in their stories, and much of the parent's experiences were focused on their children's lives. This means I gathered information about many peoples' experiences, beyond the nine participants interviewed. The participants' stories only make sense when they aligned them with the stories of others. The expansive nature of people's experiences has been explained by other authors in poverty literature (Dean, 2009, pp. 268–269), paying respect to the insights of Ubuntu; a person is a person through other people (Eze, 2010, pp. 190–191). Poverty is relational; the nine participants' experiences are not

TABLE 5.1 Participant Demographics

Participant	*Gender*	*Age*	*Payments*	*Employment*	*Education*	*Family*	*Housing*	*Transport*	*Health*	*Participation*
Teresa	F	Early 50s	Newstart	Part time and gigs	Attended tertiary	Siblings Pets	Public	Both	On-going issues	Intermittent Extensive
Sandra	F	Mid30s	Parenting Payment Single to Newstart	Student	Tertiary going back to university	Single mother with boyfriend	Private rent	Private (car)	Major illness	Constant Extensive
Adam	M	Early 20s	Newstart	Unemployed to work for the dole to temporary work	Highschool looking to university	Siblings	Private rent to temporary	Public	General	Constant Extensive
Michael	M	Mid50s	Disability Support Pension	Unemployed to gig work	Postgraduate	Divorced, lives with parents	With family	Both	General	Intermittent Limited
William	M	Late 30s	Disability Support Pension	Unemployed with personal projects	Highschool to personal study	Disconnected from family	Private rent	Public	Injuries	Intermittent Short term
Charlotte	F	Early 20s	Youth Allowance	Student to part-time work	Honours graduate	Connected to mother	Private rent	Public	General	Constant Extensive
Natalie	F	Early 30s	Newstart	Student with gig work	Completing undergraduate	Connected to parents	Private rent	Private	Chronic	Constant Extensive
Emily	F	Early 30s	Parenting Payment Single to Newstart	Student with part-time work	Completing postgraduate (masters)	Single mother ,Siblings	Private rent	Unknown	General	Intermittent Limited
Donna	F	Late 50s	Disability Support Pension	Unemployed with personal projects	Undergraduate	Single mother	Private rent	Private	Injuries	Constant Extensive

generalisable but are transferable patterns at a societal level (see Hodgetts & Stolte, 2017; Hodgetts et al., 2019).

Poverty as a Contextual Experience

What was poverty like for these participants? I never sought to collate a shared definition of poverty. I wanted each of my participants to speak out their perspectives on poverty. So below is each case of my participants' experience of poverty summarised.

Pets as Family

Teresa, a middle-aged woman who had been in an out of poverty and support systems all her life without prompting, gave me an answer to 'what is poverty?'. "Poverty is owning a horse" if said by someone in a wealthier position would be laughable for many, but with Teresa a focus on animals defined a lot of our conversations. Teresa, in her youth, did know some measure of comfort, owning a horse, but still today, she needs money because of her love of animals. She tried to pursue her animal-based passions in education only to be blocked by poverty. Without other family, Teresa's pets were the centre of her life. This love is juxtaposed with others dismissing pets' importance, treating pets as luxuries, or not understanding why you would spend money to keep them alive and healthy. Poverty for Teresa was a missing passion, a fight to keep a family, and a misunderstanding by those who too easily dismissed her family.

Teresa: *And [pets in poverty] is something that I would like to tackle. With the backing where, I see having the organisations and getting people to come forward and getting people to say that housing trust needs to accept that [pets are important] … Especially people that are going to be alone in a single room flat. They need something else there, and a really good one is a companion animal. A pet, and yes, we cannot let them have a million pets I understand that! They will say that regardless. They will always say that.* ***But they shouldn't have control over a person's family. Pets are family, they shouldn't have control over it!***

While participating in the group, an event explored having pets in poverty. There I listened to stories of those in poverty being told to "put down" (euthanise) their pets as budget control. Attendants, through their teeth or tears spoke of high surrender fees at adoption centres and even higher vet bills for euthanasia. To others, pets were luxury 'items' rather than mental health supports, responsibilities, and family members.

Poverty Is the Absence of Hope

Sandra: *Yeah … [poor people] have all lost hope as well too. That is half the problem.* ***And I think hope is the keyword****, I think hope is absolutely the keyword because that is the one thing that you are, that you all have, that when you are pulling together that you hope for a better day, hope for things to change, hope for life to begin to get better.*

Sandra, a mother of two young children, was often stuck at home reading or watching the media stigmatise the poor. Sandra wished that such attention could instead help people. Sandra spoke about "resonating very well with Katie", a character depicting struggling motherhood in the movie *I, Daniel Blake* (2016). Sandra used that resonance and the group to combat poverty by providing hope for change. Sandra grew up in a low-income family before being relatively well off within her marriage, to going through "the worst time in [her] life", or in her terms, ending up "dirt poor". Sandra wanted stability for her children, a pathway out of poverty through education, and in the community group solidarity, camaraderie, and hope.

Sandra: *It's knowing that there are other people out there facing the same problem as you. That are willing to fight it too like you. You are not the only person standing up, you are not the only person, standing up and going this is wrong!*

Am I Poor? Do I Have Purpose?

Adam: *The fact of the matter is I'm fucking fine. I feel kind of bad talking to you here because I'm comfortable in the money that I get. I can live on it. I can save up. The only reason I don't spend as much as I do is because it can get cut off at any time.*

As a young, self-improvement focus man, Adam gave a direct definition of poverty, poverty is not affording the necessary resources, but as a necessity, he includes purpose.

Adam: *If I was to define poverty as "just poverty" then I would say "the inability to be able to pay for your necessities* ***and*** *some form of entertainment" … That is why people they always say that welfare is meant to be able to make you pay for the necessities but define these necessities.* ***What the fuck*** *is a necessity?! Things like shelter, food, and water, if you want to live but if you live on an island you need to get shelter, get food, and find water, or grow food, and set a water system up somehow with bamboo and all that weird shit!* ***But*** *that will give you* ***a sense of purpose*** *because you need to act to give* *yourself, to survive but in this situation, it's like okay you have the money you spend the money. You know, that is why-*

Eden: *No fulfilment?*

Adam: ***No purpose!***

Adam allows everyone to define their purpose differently, saying that he would support Work for the Dole if it gave someone that sense of purpose. There was an inescapable theme for Adam that if he were not to achieve something and quickly, there would be no hope for where he could go (travel), what he could do (career), and whom he could have relationships with (partnership). Adam avoided eating and constantly saved to be prepared for later bills. For Adam, then poverty was about the future and potential losses that poverty led him towards, being alone and purposeless.

Educated View of Poverty

Michael, as a middle-aged man with a high level of education, avoided poverty as a subject. Instead, due to his extreme knowledge of socio-political-economic history, Michael focused on the extensive patterns, effects, and shifts in society. He pointed out structural elements, including the welfare system's obligations, particularly Work for the Dole, to highlight how such programmes suppressed everyone's wages through competition in the labour market. Poverty and the systems that constrained Michael were inseparable from the capitalist system, which he viewed as working as intended. Poverty is part of the structure and intentional.

Michael: ***Everyone knows you have a shit time on Centrelink.*** *The government designed it to be a shit time. The government they intend it. The government is saying all these people are having a shit time on Centrelink well "Oh, it's working" ... but they go "Oh, this is a shit time" it's supposed to be, you should feel bad about being on Centrelink.*

Transient Poverty

William, as a well-travelled man in his 30s, had extreme experiences of crime, homelessness, and churning between working and being poor. He described poverty as a transitional state with an analogy of being on the edge of a cliff.

William: *Okay, let's go with a cliff analogy* ***in poverty you stand on the edge of that cliff and the wind is against you non-fucking-stop.***

Eden: *And the next step is dead?*

William: *Well, it can be. With self-harm there is the chance of dead. The brightest outlook of the fall is serious harm, you know? That even though you are standing on the edge of the cliff and being blown over the cliff is a scary prospect; the bottom is always worse than where you are now! At the beach to the cliff there is a nice winding staircase to get back up. But the social system, is that you will climb the rockface, and now the winds are against you again and you have got breakers on your back, you are not getting back up from it!*

William thought many people could be considered poor due to their precarious economic situation – not falling yet. William had some praise for government and non-government agencies helping those in poverty, who had fallen off the cliff, but felt they were ultimately a façade: "One spray of air freshener in a public toilet". This view of poverty as a precipice included the efforts of those in power acting against poor people, which for William motivated personal projects to grow his own food and build his own shelter. William was trying to be self-sufficient, get out of the game, get off the cliff.

Effort Is Not Rewarded

Charlotte, a young woman taking every opportunity for education and self-reliance, like Adam before, questioned how poor she was; she could feed herself and live alone, despite the stress and limitations caused by her financial situation. Charlotte separated the poor and non-poor as "not having to work to death to achieve the bare minimum". Charlotte could easily be described as the participant with the best prospects and the most success on their current pathways out of poverty, taking many volunteering, employment, and educational opportunities even when this high effort for little reward was detrimental to her mental health. This was balanced against her and the group knowing that effort, and ability, do not always mean reward.

Charlotte: *I technically am well below the poverty line or whatever. But I am thinking I am doing pretty fine. I have food and I have a house, and that, so I am like yeah "I'm not that poor?" ... I think poverty is a technical thing. Like, you are below this threshold so, you can't do certain things or do certain things that other people can. But more, of a crisis situation as well*

Eden: *So, like the psychological element in there as well?*

Charlotte: *Yeah, yeah. I think so because when you are pretty stressed about "can I afford food", or whatever, or "can I pay my bills" and not have someone on my back about a debt or something.* ***Then that is poverty, to me on a level. Also, the thing of being exploited. So, that thing where you take that really badly paying work.***

Charlotte had many stories of herself, or others being exploited. She explained that sometimes it is just how you get by; you take anything you can. Other times she was less complacent, exploitation burned against her sensibilities and her passion for change.

It Is No Money

Natalie, a woman in her 30s, had churned in and out of poverty over time, and she was the only participant to focus consistently on limited income.

Natalie: *So! I would define it as not having enough money to comfortably live without worry. To me poverty is in the background.* ***It's the issue, money dominates every facet of your life,*** *and I think when you're in, you* <u>*are*</u> *in poverty when you can't comfortably afford the basic necessities, that give you a life that is not miserable. So, you could have a roof over your head, and food, but I think you can still be in poverty! Because if you are constantly terrified of the electricity bill, so, you don't have the electricity on that means you get cold. I think that is poverty, but you might have a roof over your head, and you can still be grateful of the things you have but be in poverty. I would probably also describe it as I would go the opposite as well like you are not in poverty when you don't have to think about every minute purchase. So, you would be able to go somewhere and be like "that looks nice" and its 10 dollars then you can make a decision quickly. I spend ridiculous amounts of time agonising over purchases. I'm already an indecisive person, when I am at a shop and I am like "Oh, I'm not sure whether I should get this do I not" and I can be there for 10 or 20 minutes. Someone who is not in poverty would be "Oh whatever!" and then if they don't like it or whatever then it's not a big deal. But for me, I agonise over small purchases. So, I think that is poverty, if you agonise over getting something for 10 dollars, I think you are in poverty.*

Money was central but the psychological stress was about control. As we spoke, Natalie's stress was, like in other literature, particularly created by strangers. Frontline workers who argued with Natalie over her educational aspirations because of her disability (see Humpage, 2007). Or friends and colleagues lost when they argued that countries like Australia do not have poverty and 'real poverty' was secluded to the developing world. Natalie spoke of her reliance on eating bland, cheap food that ultimately meant she was deprived. Her poverty was limited resources but also the need to fight for recognition as a poor person. Natalie spoke of her poverty not as destitution but focused on the psychological and social experiences of stress, worry, and exclusion by others. This definition would include many people above the poverty line, some with rather expensive lifestyles because at its centre is socio-psychological distress and identity.

Rights to the Bare Minimum

Emily, a young single mother, worried for providing and living well with her son, focused her perspective on the issue of necessities and rights.

Emily: *Because to me, poverty is linked to, inextricably linked to problems of living. I don't want to sound reductionist or anything, but it is, and for me the aim of [the community group] is to have levels of subsistence that we deserve, [are] entitled to, as a minimum, as a bare minimum! ...* ***it's, to me, about creating subsistence level that people have rights and living standards.***

Eden: *Like the poverty line shouldn't be what we are striving to attain for people it should be the* <u>*rock bottom*</u> *you can possibly get to?*

Emily: *Yeah, but also, it's not about this kind of sort of moral ethical standard it's very much about friendships and lives.*

Emily, like Michael, spoke from a position of knowledge, well versed in sociological theory and the arguments of disadvantage. Emily spoke about poverty as something many people could not understand without experience. Still, she thought these issues could be solved rather easily. She argued against the solution being the powerful social class benevolently providing resources to those with less. Instead, she spoke of redistribution, focused on relationships. Poverty for her was the intersection with social relationships and identity, especially with gendered social reproduction, which, for her, meant her identity conflicts as a mother, worker, student, and activist.

It Is about Life Not Poverty

Donna, an older woman with adult children, like Michael, never made any direct comments that told me what she thought poverty was as a standalone concept. She often spoke of how the lack of money led to poor housing conditions, her relationships, her isolation, her mental health status, and the follow-on effects for her children. Donna commented directly on the churning nature of her constraints.

Donna: *No, it's like I was saying before having had a comfortable life and* ***then all of a sudden being put into you know abject poverty,*** *I couldn't even pay the bills, it's like I know things always start being alright and then boom something always happens*

Like everyone else, Donna could not avoid the permeating nature of money troubles into every aspect of life despite the money focus being rare in conversations, she still in a matter-of-fact way told me, "Life goes fine when you have got that money, but as soon as you are in the hole it just cycles and you just [trails off] ...".

In Summary

I have no final answer for 'what is poverty?'. The community group never settled on one idea of poverty. I never uniformly asked what poverty is, instead I put these summaries together as they arose throughout conversations.

Suppose a similar method was carried out for a larger number of people. In that case, it is expected that many people would fall into a category like Donna, for who no sections of conversations are coded as definitions or explanations of 'what poverty is'. I would expect that many would be like some of my participants definitions and other definitions would appear. A more important analysis was on when and how people used definitions of poverty.

Functions of Multiple Definitions

There are several threads in these descriptions, but they are contextually bound definitions. Participants avoided stating that any one item, object, or activity absolutely made someone poor or not. There are several possible functions for avoiding strict definitions, for example:

- Speaking this way functions to maintain members' status as 'someone in poverty' despite churning above and below thresholds or 'feeling fine'.
- Speaking this way lets you agree or disagree with others' definitions as they arise.
- Speaking this way is the only amenable answer to an otherwise absurd question: 'what is poverty?'.

The second point above is important as quite often when poverty was spoken about in groups multiple audiences were present who *required* fluid definitions of poverty. When speaking to politicians for a raise to benefits, there must be a focus on income, money, and expenses – missing out by being unable to afford their needs. In other cases, such as the community group, the notions of hope and solidarity are more valuable because they encourage exchange without money as the medium. At other times there are wants and desires that seemed to invite criticism. For example, Teresa wanting a horse while others may discount this as luxury.

But asking poor people what poverty is, is absurd. People cannot answer what poverty is fundamentally, answers to this question are not absolute, but rather functionally do something to other people (Guerin, 1994, 2016). To expect any individual to generate an accurate answer which takes into consideration general or average reality assumes they know the experience for everyone else in the population. This is ludicrous. The answer is always bound to contexts and consequences of what is said. Questions arise; who is asking? Why do you want to know? It should be unsurprising we have abstract, disconnected but generalisable answers. Those answers are hard to challenge, they are difficult to dispute, and they can be used to help people live with a little less stress.

Shared Experiences

Stability

The churning in and out of poverty was constant. Any relationship or resource management today was preparation for issues coming tomorrow. Issues were relational; a roommate leaving water running and now there is a huge bill (Sandra, William); ending of a partnership or marriage and losing their resources (Sandra, Adam, Michael, Emily); or children and pets you desperately hide poverty from (Teresa, Sandra, Charlotte, Emily, Donna). The latter was particularly gendered. These downturns were expected but unpredictable. Some downturns were more violent than others, but everyone had plans for when it would all go wrong. Conversely participants spoke of possible new relationships as avenues to economic stability.

Effects on Mental Health

Instability produced anxiety. Participants did not know what will happen next but expected it to be bad. Without the community group, many members experienced isolation. Frontline workers of health, bureaucracy, and other services were catalysts for worsened mental health. House cleaners criticised Teresa and a food bank employee refused her the toilet, insinuating she was a criminal. Michael found his psychologist unhelpful. William felt psychologists needed to "open their ears". Charlotte's psychologist told her "Others have it worse". A JSP worker interrogated Natalie's ability to complete university if she had a disability. Emily did constant care work for her ex-husband's mental health issues. These are a tiny hint of the everyday mental health struggles – stressors that cannot go away with a change in mindset.

Strangers who spoke to community group members endlessly gave banal and rather stupid suggestions for poor people to 'help themselves'. From politicians at the state or local level to random people at events simplistic answers were given; start your own business, just get a job, change your outlook, or "I know what it is like and look at me now" survivorship bias. If

Teresa just cleaned her own house, if Adam were just less anxious, if Donna just moved in with strangers, if poor people just got a job, then they each would improve their mental health issues and socio-economic position. The issue is the circularity of the argument; if you did more you would have less to do. These simplistic answers make poverty a private issue, avoiding social responsibility – "Oh, you can give me a job then?".

Purpose

All participants pointed to some activity, hobby, or career that would provide purpose. Education was often touted as the key to get out of poverty, but education failed many. The community often laughed at the notion of a meritocracy or just world. Many group conversations centred on how the only way to get out of poverty was to accept a bad job and a purposeless life – poverty by another measure. But we all know, purpose, and meaningfulness in work, are key to well-being (Haar et al., 2018).

Again, relationships were key, Charlotte had a well-paying job she was passionate about, but a bad boss resulted in her leaving, something others labelled an error or irrational. Others took on volunteering, finding meaningfulness through helping each other. Helping others can be meaningful but does not solve income poverty (Allan et al., 2014). Burn out was common and helping each other ultimately meant no change in economic conditions.

A trilemma came into sharp focus. We all know the classic pick-two: a social life, enough sleep, or enough money. There is another: earn money, meaningful work, and mental health. How many of us would say that we get one of those three? Sometimes underpaid work, in poor conditions, doing menial tasks, is all job searches turn up. Work for work's sake cannot be the answer, despite politicians' dictations, a bad job can be worse than no job at all (Chandola & Zhang, 2018).

Do Not Focus on Money

Beside Natalie, other participants spoke more on the topics of work, effort, and social relationships. Money, however, remains the 'middleman' of poverty. A focus on money limits our understanding of hardship and we need new frameworks, such as *Social–Financial Connectedness* (Snow et al., 2017, p. 354). Participants problems of living are often separate from money (Collins, 2005). Money is easy to measure and compare, while idiosyncratic abstractions are hard (Belk & Wallendorf, 1990; Zelizer, 1994, 2010). Still, for the community there were a few possible reasons for avoiding poverty being "all about money":

1. A focus on money can be scornful. Focusing on getting money seemed at odds with the community groups' purpose: hope through solidarity. One group member suggested taking opportunities out of poverty, such as scholarships, were avoided because "we [poor people] don't do that" choosing to stay with family to provide support. Similar rejections of money as a focus were seen in Verdouw's (2017) group of *downshifters*, those who exit from the 'rat race' of careers and money. Downshifters' exits were, however, facilitated by succeeding financially. Regardless, increasing economic resources is only one goal out of many (Henrich et al., 2001, p. 77). The result is detaching 'earning more' from the notion of 'a good life'.

2. Disposability of social relationships. Money was used by some to end social relationships: if I pay you for something then I expect the exchange to be discrete or singular like a stranger in a shop. If someone offered food, and the receiver paid with money, then the receiver does not need to give food or other resources later. In this case, exchanges and relationships are curtailed. If you use money, you do not generalise the exchange to other times, people, or behaviours (Guerin, 2016). Relationships come with many other obligations that may be more problematic for people in poverty than it seems on the surface.

3. Balancing effortfulness against being an acceptable worker-citizen. Poor people need a balance between the effort they put in, or report verbally, and their claim of needing more resources to live comfortably (Gibson, 2009). Poor people cannot overstress the virtue of earning more via work, especially given many of them had been in detrimental, exploitative, or purposeless work in the past. Money alone cannot provide the more esoteric and affective outcomes of a good life. Bad work would solve the income problem. Instead, people were advocating for a stable and comfortable life, while rejecting employment as the core responsibility. Avoid talking about money, and you avoid the inevitable "there are plenty of jobs" claim, blaming people in poverty as inept worker-citizens.

Interconnections

There are big lists of indicators of poverty. These appeared in my data, all entangled and interconnected. This is hopefully unsurprising. While I analysed for this, participants also spoke of interconnection (Table 5.2).

Community group events made the breadth of interconnections clear. Events were held about pets, drugs, illness, homelessness, prisons, unemployment, refugee status, educational opportunities, dental care, mental health, public housing, renters' rights, and electricity prices. These conversations moved to privatisation, transport costs, raising the rate of Newstart, Youth Allowance, and other related pensions.

TABLE 5.2 Interconnection Examples from Participant Talk

Participant	*Interconnections*
Teresa	"... everything interacts or impacts with everything else"
Sandra	"[People ask] 'Alright what are the main things affecting you?' It would branch out to everything! It really does!"
Adam	On relationships, the future, and purpose to poverty "that is going onto another point completely"
Michael	Everything was systemic interconnections, e.g., attempting to get a job is alienating him from himself "everyone does it, well all these people!"
William	Survival means an interconnection between low income, social skills, mental health, and his need to complete personal projects (shelter and food)
Charlotte	*C:* "[It] All plays in together" E: "It's all poverty related?" *C:* "Yeah, it's all poverty"
Natalie	"It just permeates just every facet of your life, not having enough money"
Emily	"... some people will dissect they will take race, class, gender, and everything and try to separate them and individualise them but for me, you can't do that"
Donna	Going from being well-off to poverty, accommodation troubles, social isolation, fear, ill health, and future worries

> The class of the poor, especially in modern society, is a unique sociological synthesis. It possesses a great homogeneity insofar as its meaning and location in the social body is concerned, but it lacks it completely insofar as the individual qualification of its elements is concerned. It is the common end of the most diverse destinies, an ocean into which lives derived from the most diverse social strata flow together.
>
> *(Simmel, 1908/1965, p. 139)*

The quote above provides a reliable description of the current conclusion. The only similarity for group members is that they come together as a group. Poverty is not what binds them, poverty is made of entangling and intertwining constraints. Though different, through the community group, these people come together in solidarity as 'the poor' with only their anxiety over their problematic situation to bind them.

Premiums and Catch-22s

Poverty costs you, stuck between a rock and a hard place, and needing preparation for things to get worse. People were often avoiding help because they could be blamed for their situation. Some of the choices that come from this were detrimental but understandable. Live alone and pay everything yourself, live with others and they may produce higher costs. These choices are irrational from a mathematical point of view but on the ground, they are reasonable preparations.

Catch-22s and poverty premiums were well understood in the group. The group and its members shared SACOSS's (2017) statistics: poor people suffer 328% higher cost of telecommunications technology, 28% more for electricity due to delayed payment, and 2.5 times more of their disposable income goes to food compared to richer people. Stability was the goal but the catch-22s broke it. That big bill or a payment cut-off can wipe you out ending in "a damned if you do, damned if you don't" situation around saving and spending. All my participants felt the bite of these constraints (Table 5.3).

TABLE 5.3 Catch-22's of Constraints Experienced by Participants

Participant	*Catch-22*
Teresa	Temporarily lost internet at home while applying for financial services assistance. Using the library lost her privacy but mobile data was too expensive. "I have no internet and can't use the phone ... I am savvy with money"
Sandra	Chose not to work more and earn money to focus on her failing health. "I knew I was stuffing up, in the sense that I should have been taking my vitamins. I should have been taking medicine from my doctor, but I just couldn't afford it"
Adam	Constantly questioning if going to university to improve his skills was worth his time if a job is not guaranteed either
Michael	Questioned reaching out to old colleagues to ask for assistance and the stress induced by that act. Perfectionism had harmed his career but felt needed for success.
William	Expectations of behaviour for a good life, working an ordinary job, and worsening his mental health which made him unsuitable for most workplaces
Charlotte	Took jobs and sacrificed her mental health and choosing between working and helping her mother (choosing work could harm her relationship with other family)
Natalie	Pursuing her disability pension applications came with an expectation of ceasing her efforts at education and employment. "I am I supposed to not study then? Because am I not allowed to study because I'm poor? I don't have the right to an education"
Emily	Chose taking on new roles in activism and ultimately not being able to fulfil all the needs of those in the group. "This structural thing that I'm always butting my head against it, and I'm like I can't do anything. What can I do? Am I making the wrong decisions. I am constantly reassessing what I do"
Donna	Choosing between living alone, without her children for financial support, but had no money. At the same time would not ask them to stay – never wanting to "rock the boat".

Employment was not a solution as it came with precarity (Rua et al., 2019; Standing, 2011). Taking on work with poor conditions, minimum wage pay despite qualifications, or missing out socially due to work and the care of children, all result in poorer mental health and stress.

Social Relationships as Stressful

Social relationships, especially the power of stranger relationships, are captured in previous research. Teresa was confronted for needing a toilet while at a food bank, Sandra, Natalie, and Emily's study was interrogated by others. This is before we discuss the media and general population constantly critiquing the choices and behaviour of poor people. Positives from relationships came with a bitter taste. Michael lived with parents to maintain some stability but is an older man with post-graduate qualifications, so he worried it was shameful. William moved interstate to avoid harmful relationships but ended up largely alone. Several of the single mothers left abusive relationships only to be thrown into poverty.

'Relying on family' is so complicated. For example, Michael's parents were a positive force, while Charlotte's were more a source of instability or distress. Adam and Donna were disconnected from family. Family, therefore, as a category produces exceptionally different observable realities for participants. All relationships, family, friends, and strangers come with positives and negatives, but ultimately sustaining relationships is a struggle in poverty – because you cannot exchange much, without much to give (Table 5.4).

When strangers were the issue, the actual people involved 'the girl' or 'the guy' at some institution or business, people who were name parts of institutions they represented. Institutions were confronted at local, state, and federal levels though. Public events either ended in resounding support for the group or opponents claiming they "struggled just the same" or suggesting members "just get a job", "start a business", "go to a financial counsellor", or that "free food was available". Most group members quickly recognised the political artifice placed between them and those that represented them. Often politeness was an obligation and not sincere and everyone knew it. When it broke and politicians or frontline workers came down hard, they echo the neoliberal ethos – trying to help poor people help themselves. Oddly, the most stress-inducing element was after these events, after everything sounded nice, we knew no real progress was coming.

The participants also acted as relationships for one another through the community group. Most participants praised the group for its diversity and the ability to welcome all people affected by poverty. The group gave people hope and a sense of solidarity.

Donna: *Having been with [the group] I feel it makes me feel more powerful that we can change something*

TABLE 5.4 Important Social Relationships Mentioned by Participants

Participant	*Mentioned social relationships*
Teresa	• Pets, animals, and related social groups • Workmates and customer services • Lack of children • Welfare bureaucracy • Expectation not to be social
Sandra	• Children and family support • New partner support • Group support • Strangers keeping her from working
Adam	• Loss of key familial relationships • Future partnership • Pet as a positive • Focus on improving social skills
Michael	• Effects of lost relationships on mental health • Worries for the future (partner, parents, children) • Music community connection • Workplace community disconnection
William	• Move to new city (new relationships, loss of old relationships) • Roommate • Community participation (poetry events) • Other species
Charlotte	• Mother–family obligations • Group relationships • Working relationship troubles • Poverty reducing exit from intimate relationships
Natalie	• Government by policy • Media by presentation of poor • Strangers • car crash, landlord company, frontline workers
Emily	• Child • Ex-partner (care work) • Fictive kin • Children's school and hobby networks • Positive relationships with landlord and boss
Donna	• Children • History with ex-partners • Helpful and unhelpful mental and medical care professionals • Strangers impacting living (real estate, car crashes, avoiding bureaucracy)

Preparing for the Worst

With problematic relationships, catch-22s and general instability, participants were expecting sudden shocks. Many expectations were virtual – stories they told themselves that were not 'really' happening to them but affecting them all the same (Guerin, 2015, pp. 65–95). Teresa worried about monitoring by welfare agencies, especially when her housing was controlled by a new company. Adam avoided eating to be ready for future shocks. Natalie's activism was to stop control going to income management programmes. Donna stressed about her children getting older, awake through the night worrying about how she could live well on her own. None of these things were happening yet but preparation was. Panic attacks, anxiety, insomnia, and avoidance of pleasure all were part of that preparation.

The most worrying spectre was Robodebt. Robodebts were debts sent out via an automated system to welfare recipients whose tax records showed a mismatched between what they earned in previous years and the amount they were entitled to in welfare payments. They would need to repay the gap or prove they did not owe the money. Since the end of my research, a Royal Commission into Robodebts has found the programme to be illegal and erroneous (Holmes, 2023). Only a tiny number of group members received a debt letter during the study. But only knowing it was possible was enough to keep many others awake at night and scared during the day, saving what they could waiting for that letter saying they owed it all back.

Stress and Habit

Experimental stress in psychology is momentary, in reality stress is constant and multi-levelled. The people I spoke to were in no position to argue back, to stop the stress, or to prepare effectively. The group members need to keep engaging in these systems for support as "the deprived are assigned to the core category of the poor only when they receive assistance" (Coser, 1965, p. 141). To be poor means to give into monitoring and remove privacy. Allowing strangers to track your behaviour, waiting for you to make a mistake, to question your deservedness and justify the removal of assistance. The worries and stressors mean you constantly need to hide your poverty and affirm it at the same time.

Previous work suggested that poor people fall back on habitual behaviour when they are stressed, but what does that behaviour look like in context? In my research the goal was not to get more income, but rather purpose, stability, and sociability.

Teresa held savings all year for a Christmas dinner with her family; she could have used this for a more durable purchase. Michael spent a lot of money on music equipment which gave him an identity, social life, and a sense of accomplishment. Donna used large legal reimbursement for holidays and hobbies for her children; she knew investing the money would be better but literally shrugged this notion off. The simple reality was that money was not a motivating factor despite knowing others expect it. I consistently found there is other meaning to economic behaviour than getting out of poverty or getting ahead economically – and this is not a new finding (Henrich et al., 2001, p. 77; de Ridder et al., 2012, p. 79; Granovetter, 1985, 2005; Zelizer, 2010). Participants were not hedonistic or gratifying themselves; they were keeping hobbies, relationships, and identity intact. They were keeping their life stable and churning effectively.

What could be called irrational behaviour was stability seeking. Every day is a struggle to not fall into the trap of 'mental illness' behaviour despite the depressing and anxiety-producing contexts. Sandra avoided her mother; Michael avoided more work; Charlotte left a well-paying job. All these things in a pure tangible or classical economic analysis speak to poor money management or habitual behaviour, but in context reveal complex planning and understanding of the pitfalls and problems of engaging in utility-maximising behaviour opposed to context-stabilising behaviour. Participants also planned to maintain resources and minimise social, cultural, and economic losses. Teresa's efforts to get cheap food and provide it even cheaper to others, Adam stopping his hobbies and saving all he could for a rainy day, and William's distaste for 'normal' working environments over his personal goals all were for stability in poverty.

Efforts to maintain a status quo could be seen as impulse, an action of the fast 'system one' cognitive system (Kahneman, 2011), an unsophisticated thought pattern based on underdeveloped, illogical, mechanics of the human mind. Motivation, willpower, and thinking style inside the person were to blame in previous psychology research. What my data suggests, however, is that participants' choices were aimed at wrestling a tiny amount of control back, to keep the few nice things they rely on, and to maintain their mental health and their social relationships which are constantly under threat from reduced resources for exchange. The opposite of rational economic behaviour is then not irrationality but socially and culturally bound behaviour.

I suggest an alternative to 'unthinking behaviour' being what maintains poverty. Many group members knew their behaviour reproduced their poverty and others did it without knowing it. Teresa disliked people who avoided assistance but when offered food rejected it, leaving the assistance for "someone else that needs it". Sandra argued for more education to end poverty, while explaining how well educated she was. Adam denied his poverty while sometimes not eating or being able to pay his rent. Michael hated work but worried that without a career he would be alone for the rest of his life. William had an aversion to authority while arguing his authority on several topics. Charlotte was working towards education and a job but disliked being recognised as working for a living. Natalie took jobs without pay because it was a "labour of love". Emily disliked the gendered imposition of care work but do it to avoid judgement. Donna worried for her future but did not "rock the boat".

These behaviours, only one example for each participant, are emblematic of the conflict between being poor and wanting change: self-defeating behaviours to maintain control in small pockets of stability, rejected help. They need to be poor to be given support, but they also just want to keep going, keep surviving.

This happens at a social level too. Participants with relationships with those in higher socio-economic positions had difficulties. Charlotte distrusted wealthier people and could not relate well to them. Donna described falling out with her wealthy friend over what it is like to struggle. The group avoided including non-poor people, while knowing they needed their support. The argumentative or discursive conflicts created tension, stress, and ultimately loss of relationships. Unfortunately, maintaining relationships with other poor people was terribly difficult because neither party has much to exchange.

Putting It All Together

We could locate these issues inside people, in their cognition (e.g., Manstead, 2018), or, as in Figure 5.1, we can rethink this cycle of poverty to be more contextual and observable with everyday social behaviour with everything discussed so far.

So, altogether the material reality of peoples' lives mandate certain ways of thinking and talking about their choices and pathways (see Chapter 7 for more). From there to protect themselves from the many threats and stressors, they try to get by with others only to lose out when they no longer have resources to draw on. This ultimately starts the cycle again, an academic like me has found poverty. Disruption, I suggest, should happen in this cycle (hopefully at the start – see Chapter 1).

Conclusions

There are many moving parts to the contextualisation of poverty. These resources, relationships, ways of getting by are so various that a chapter like this does not truly do justice to the needs and the complexities of any of these participants' lives. So, keeping these wider abstract theoretical considerations, we move to a companion piece in Chapter 6, two fuller cases of contextualising poverty: Teresa and Natalie's experiences.

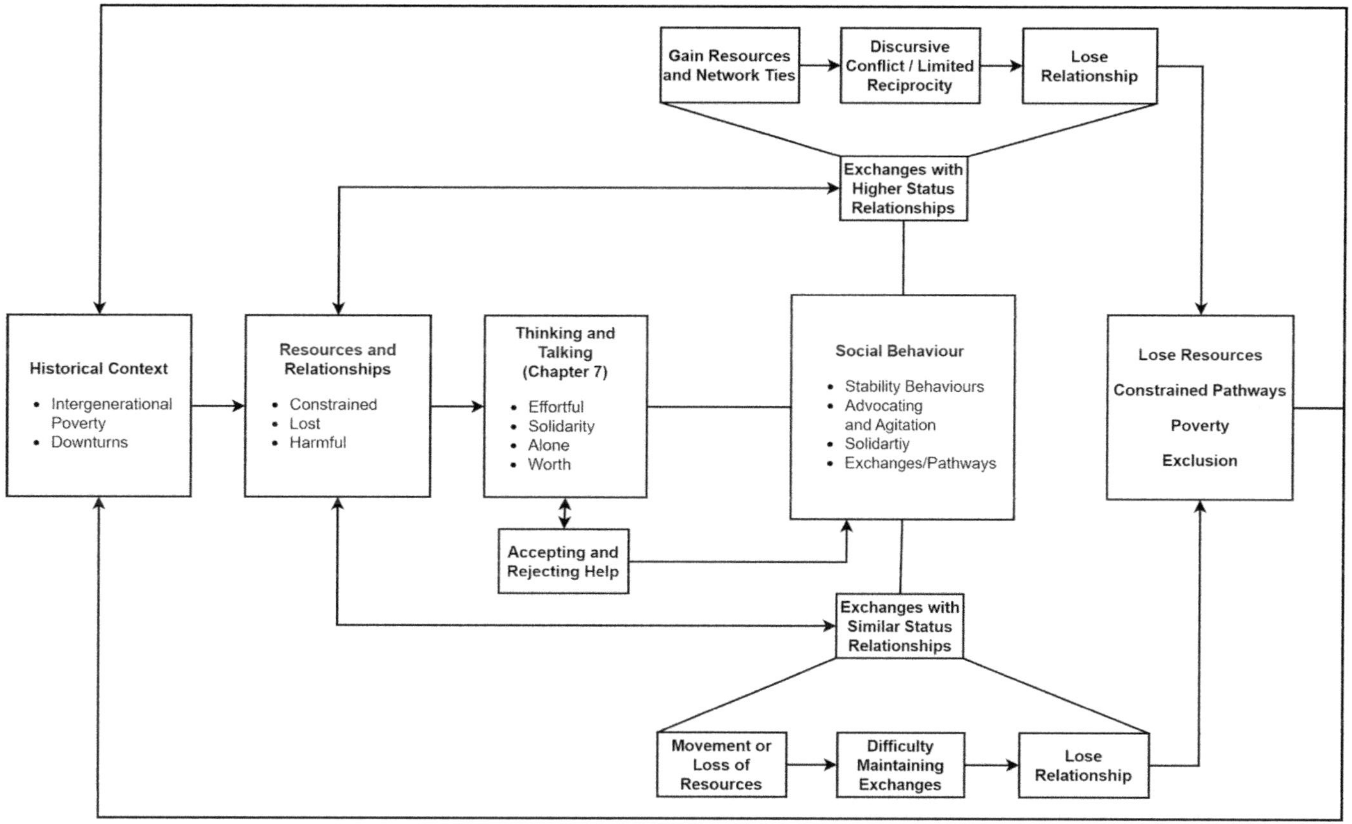

FIGURE 5.1 The social contextual cycle of getting by.

References

ACOSS. (2018). More than two-thirds of people back an increase to Newstart: Essential Poll. Australian Council of Social Services. Retrieved from: www.acoss.org.au/media_release/more-than-two-thirds-of-people-back-an-increase-to-newstart-essential-poll/

Allan, B. A., Autin, K. L., & Duffy, R. D. (2014). Examining social class and work meaning within the psychology of working framework. *Journal of Career Assessment, 22*(4), 543–561. doi:10.1177/1069072713514811

Beck, U. (2000). Living your own life in a runaway world: Individualism, globalisation and politics. In W. Hutton & A. Giddens (eds.), *On the edge: Living with global capitalism* (pp. 164–74). Vintage.

Belk, R. W., & Wallendorf, M. (1990). The sacred meanings of money. *Journal of Economic Psychology, 11*(1), 35–67. https://doi.org/10.1016/0167-4870(90)90046-C

Chandola, T., & Zhang, N. (2018). Re-employment, job quality, health and allostatic load biomarkers: Prospective evidence from the UK Household Longitudinal Study. *International Journal of Epidemiology, 47*(1), 47–57. doi:10.1093/ije/dyx150

Collins, S. B. (2005). An understanding of poverty from those who are poor. *Action Research, 3*(1), 9–31. doi:10.1177/1476750305047983

Coser, L. (1965). The sociology of poverty: To the memory of Georg Simmel. *Social Problems, 13*(2), 140–148. doi:10.2307/798899

De Ridder, D. T., Lensvelt-Mulders, G., Finkenauer, C., Stok, F. M., & Baumeister, R. F. (2012). Taking stock of self-control: A meta-analysis of how trait self-control relates to a wide range of behaviors. *Personality and Social Psychology Review, 16*(1), 76–99. https://doi.org/10.1177/1088868311418749

Dean, H. (2009). Critiquing capabilities: The distractions of a beguiling concept. *Critical Social Policy, 29*(2), 261–278. doi:10.1177/0261018308101629

Department of Social Services (DSS). (2018). *DSS payment demographic data*. https://data.gov.au/data/dataset/cff2ae8a-55e4-47db-a66d-e177fe0ac6a0

Desmond, M. (2012). Disposable ties and the urban poor. *American Journal of Sociology, 117*(5), 1295–1335. https://doi.org/10.1086/663574

Desmond, M. (2014). Relational ethnography. *Theory and Society, 43*(5), 547–579. doi:10.1007/s11186-014-9232-5

Desmond, M. (2016). *Evicted: Poverty and profit in the American city*. Broadway Books.

Eze, M. (2010). *Intellectual history in contemporary South Africa*. Springer.

Gibson, S. (2009). The effortful citizen: Discursive social psychology and welfare reform. *Journal of Community & Applied Social Psychology, 19*(6), 393–410. doi:10.1002/casp.1003

Granovetter, M. (1985). Economic action and social structure: The problem of embeddedness. *American Journal of Sociology, 91*(3), 481–510. https://doi.org/10.1086/228311

Granovetter, M. (2005). The impact of social structure on economic outcomes. *Journal of economic perspectives, 19*(1), 33–50. DOI: 10.1257/0895330053147958

Guerin, B. (1994). What do people think about the risks of driving? Implications for traffic safety interventions. *Journal of Applied Social Psychology, 24*, 994–1021. https://doi.org/10.1111/j.1559-1816.1994.tb02370.x

Guerin, B. (2015). *How to rethink psychology: New metaphors for understanding people and their behavior*. Routledge.

Guerin, B. (2016). *How to rethink human behavior: A practical guide to social contextual analysis*. Routledge.

Haar, J., Carr, S. C., Arrowsmith, J., Parker, J., Hodgetts, D., & Alefaio-Tugia, S. (2018). Escape from working poverty: Steps toward sustainable livelihood. *Sustainability, 10*(11), 4144. doi:10.3390/su10114144

Hagenaars, A. J., & Van Praag, B. M. (1985). A synthesis of poverty line definitions. *Review of Income and Wealth, 31*(2), 139–154. https://doi.org/10.1111/j.1475-4991.1985.tb00504.x

Haveman, R. H. (2001). Poverty: Measurement and analysis. In S. N. J. Smelser & P. B. Baltes (eds.), *International encyclopedia of the social and behavioral sciences* (pp. 11917–11924). Pergamon and Publishing House.

Henrich, J., Boyd, R., Bowles, S., Camerer, C., Fehr, E., Gintis, H., & McElreath, R. (2001). In search of homo economicus: Behavioral experiments in 15 small-scale societies. *American Economic Review, 91*(2), 73–78. doi:10.1257/aer.91.2.73

Hodgetts, D., & Stolte, O. (2017). *Urban poverty and health inequalities: A relational approach*. Routledge.

Hodgetts, D., Stolte, O., King, P., & Groot, S. (2019). Reproducing the general through the local: Lessons from poverty research. In C. Højholt & E. Schraube (eds.), *Subjectivity and knowledge* (pp. 157–174). Springer. https://doi.org/10.1007/978-3-030-29977-4

Holmes, C. (2023). Report of the Royal Commission into the Robodebt Scheme. Commonwealth of Australian. https://robodebt.royalcommission.gov.au/system/files/2023-07/robodebt-royal-commission-full-report.pdf

Humpage, L. (2007). Models of disability, work and welfare in Australia. *Social Policy & Administration, 41*(3), 215–231. https://doi.org/10.1111/j.1467-9515.2007.00549.x

Kahneman, D. (2011). *Thinking, fast and slow*. Macmillan.

Lemieux, A. F., & Pratto, F. (2003). Poverty and prejudice. In S . Carr & T . Sloan, (eds.), *Poverty and psychology* (pp. 147–162). Springer.

Loach, K. (2016). *I, Daniel Blake*. [Film]

Long, E. (2010). The Australian social inclusion agenda: A new approach to social policy?. *Australian Journal of Social Issues, 45*(2), 161–182. https://doi.org/10.1002/j.1839-4655.2010.tb00173.x

Manstead, A. S. (2018). The psychology of social class: How socioeconomic status impacts thought, feelings, and behaviour. *British Journal of Social Psychology, 57*(2), 267–291. doi:10.1111/bjso.12251

Mosse, D. (2010). A relational approach to durable poverty, inequality and power. *The Journal of Development Studies, 46*(7), 1156–1178. https://doi.org/10.1080/00220388.2010.487095

Murphy, J., Murray, S., Chalmers, J., Martin, S., & Marston, G. (2011). *Half a citizen: Life on welfare in Australia*. Allen & Unwin.

Polanyi, K. (1944/2001). *The great transformation: The political and economic origins of our time*. Beacon Press.

Rua, M., Hodgetts, D., Stolte, O., King, D., Cochrane, B., Stubbs, T., Karapu, R., Neha, E., Chamberlain, K., Te Whetu, T., Te Awekotuku, N., Harr, J., & Groot, S. (2019). *Precariat Maori households today* (Te Arotahi Series Paper, May 2019 No. 2). N.Z. Published by Ngā Pae o te Māramatanga New Zealand's Māori Centre of Research Excellence.

SACOSS. (2017). SACOSS anti-poverty week 2017 statement. South Australian Council of Social Service, Adelaide. Available from www.sacoss.org.au/sites/default/files/public/documents/Reports/APW%20Statements/A-P%20Week%20Statement%202017%20-%20FINAL.pdf?fbclid=IwAR1LT7JO1mEb4257yKw0f5a55QvcEp3MbpmRJFcM63fr3kPYb08Z-KxvE0s

Saunders, P., Sutherland, K., Davidson, P., Hampshire, A., King, S., & Taylor, J. (2006). *Experiencing poverty – The voices of low-income Australians: Towards new indicators of disadvantage project, Stage 1: Focus group outcomes*. Social Policy Research Centre, University of New South Wales.

Sharam, A., & Hulse, K. (2014). Understanding the nexus between poverty and homelessness: Relational poverty analysis of families experiencing homelessness in Australia. *Housing, Theory and Society, 31*(3), 294–309. doi:10.1080/14036096.2014.882405

Simmel, G. (1903/1950). The metropolis and mental life. In K. H. Wolff (Ed.), The *Sociology of Georg Simmel* (pp. 409–424). New York: The Free Press.

Simmel, G. (1907/1971). 'Exchange' [translated extract from *Philosophie des Geldes*. Leipzig, Duncker & Humbolt.] in G. Simmel, *On individuality and social form* (pp. 43–69). University of Chicago Press.

Simmel, G. (1908/1950). The Stranger. In K. H. Wolff (Ed.), The *Sociology of Georg Simmel* (pp. 402–408). New York: The Free Press.

Small, M. L. (2009). 'How many cases do I need?' On science and the logic of case selection in field-based research. *Ethnography, 10*(1), 5–38. doi:10.1177/1466138108099586

Snow, S., Vyas, D., & Brereton, M. (2017). Sharing, saving, and living well on less: Supporting social connectedness to mitigate financial hardship. *International Journal of Human–Computer Interaction, 33*(5), 345–356. doi:10.1080/10447318.2016.1243846

Standing, G. (2011). *The precariat: The new dangerous class*. Bloomsbury Academic.

Thain, A. (2020). *Rethinking poverty: A qualitative study of becoming resource and relationship constrained in South Australia*. Unpublished PhD Thesis. University of South Australia. https://hdl.handle.net/11541.2/144892

Townsend, P. (1979). *Poverty in the United Kingdom: A survey of household resources and standards of living*. University of California Press.

Verdouw, J. J. (2017). The subject who thinks economically? Comparative money subjectivities in neoliberal context. *Journal of Sociology, 53*(3), 523–540. doi:10.1177/1440783316662717

Zambrano, E. (2014). An axiomatization of the human development index. *Social Choice and Welfare, 42*(4), 853–872. doi:10.1007/s00355-013-0756-9

Zelizer, V. (1994). *The social meaning of money*. Basic Books.

Zelizer, V. A. (2010). *Economic lives: How culture shapes the economy*. Princeton University Press.

Zelizer, V. A. (2012). How I became a relational economic sociologist and what does that mean?. *Politics & Society, 40*(2), 145–174. https://doi.org/10.1177/0032329212441591

6

PATHWAYS IN POVERTY

I would adore taking you through every one of my participants' pathways for resources and relationships. Unfortunately, a book has its limits and lends itself more to the amalgamated form in Chapter 5. None the less I need to show you at least two people's real contexts. You cannot spend the amount of time I did, almost ever, but learning from cases helps see variety from commonality (see Thain, 2020, for more). When you stay with one person, you find those sticking points, points of stress, and contextual reasons for poverty churning. Giving thought to these processes would be helpful in clinical and service provision settings. Often all that is asked for is to be more understanding of everyday realities.

Below, Teresa and Natalie's experiences are rather emblematic of what I saw constantly. Money featured well in their pathways as did interaction with the bureaucracy. The unemployment income support payment they rely on below – 'Newstart' – was well below the poverty line (Davidson et al., 2020). Just below \$40 a day or \$280 a week, an amount which remained stagnant for over 25 years (Whiteford, 2016). After the research period, a welcomed but temporary increase came during the 2020 COVID-19 crisis accompanied by politicians, of both sides, claiming the increase was "unsustainable", "a disincentive" to work, and that keeping the higher rate was "not a reasonable proposition" (Crowe, 2020; Duke, 2020). We all know full well that welfare systems fall short but here I want to tell you what they fall short of: the combination of low-income, under or unemployment, health complains, education limitations, mental health problems, and poor treatment by others in society.

DOI: 10.4324/9781003453970-6

Teresa

Teresa was a single woman in her 40s, receiving Newstart allowance, and working part-time while taking on odd casual jobs. At the time, Teresa was likely in the most common demographic of Newstart recipients according to DSS statistics (2018): female, over 40, part-time employment, with limited work hours. Her pathways in poverty, centring on money, had many key resources and relationships linked together (Figure 6.1).

Teresa was the recipient of a reduced Newstart payment. She was relieved to rarely interact with frontline welfare workers. Her other source of income was from her consistent shift work, sometimes supplemented with gigs usually found on social media groups. Teresa spoke often of the balance between more working hours and the money lost in her Newstart payment, ultimately making her hourly wage rather low for an often-straining job. The strain was an issue due to consistent health issues, a major factor keeping her yearly income below the poverty line.

Teresa: *Four hours a week with [part-time employment] through [the year]. It's like whatever comes up, you know? I look on the website on a regular basis and it's like "Oh yay, [special event] that means more [money]", [another event] in February that means a shift, [another event means] an extra shift, you hear something on the radio, you know, "Excellent that will be a bonus four hours!"*

Eden: *But then what happens when there isn't one?*

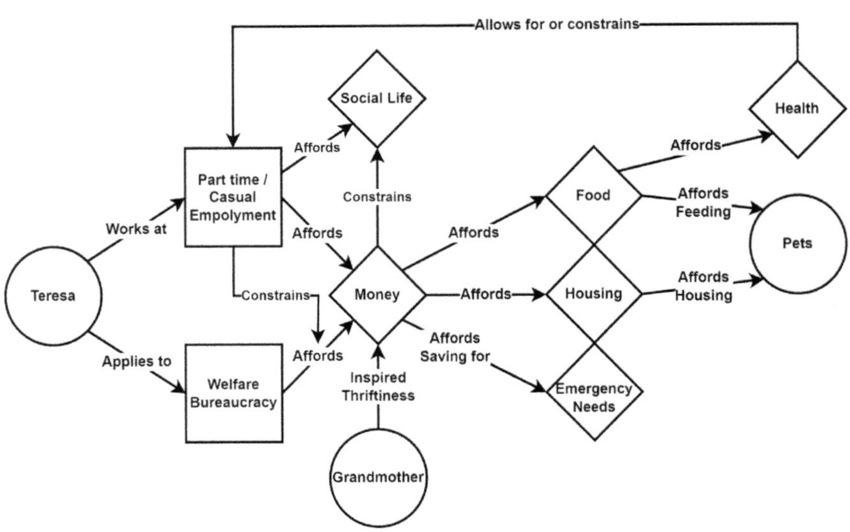

FIGURE 6.1 Teresa's pathways in poverty.

Teresa: *Well, it's just like "Oh, that's a bit of extra money" but it's not even extra money because once I earn that first 100 dollars for a fortnight [I lose] 50 cents in a dollar and housing trust want 25% of it. So, out of $200, I might get $125.*

As Teresa brought in 'extra money', she was anxious about constant monitoring.

Teresa: *[The frontline worker] was saying "Oh so we have your accounts here and there is a deposit here on this day for 100 dollars. A cheque for 100 dollars, what was that for?" and I said "Well as you will see that was around the time of my birthday. My father sent me some money for my birthday. I thought I didn't have to declare a gift!" and she said "No, you don't." The fact [is] I know how to answer that question but no! If they have any cause to think that you are doing something that you [shouldn't]… is why I lay awake at night.* ***This is not unreal; this is actually happening****!*

In the community I constantly hear worries about complicated reporting systems and data matching for income. Many discussions were strategies to deal with the scrutiny by frontline workers.

Such cross examination, and suspicion, is rarely allayed by good deeds of the past nor did it allow for stability. Teresa had a long work history, including education in her passions. Teresa remained in low-paid work, with high work ethic and pride.

Teresa: *While working … we weren't so busy, so, I do, I find something about people that I can complement them on. Or just something nice and it makes it a much more pleasant experience.*

Some of her work history included informal economic activity. At the time of interviews these were no longer her main form of income, but she spoke fondly about those times as work like any other. Despite a long and hardworking history, she was still in a position with very little for herself, her effort rarely directly rewarded. This still occurred in her current employment.

Teresa: *[Talking about bosses] Yeah, it's like you don't give the little people credit for, you know?*
Eden: *Doing the hard work? The groundwork?*
Teresa: *Yeah. It wasn't even hard work it was just like the caring work.*

Work also provided a social outlet and a source of solidarity for Teresa.

Teresa: *I have said before like work is a little bit social in the sense of like I build those work friendships with people … I have said that they are family.*

Outside work and the community group, Teresa did not have many other connections. She occasionally went to bars as her 'social life" but said often that poor people are not expected to have a social life.

Teresa: *… you know I suppose being involved in the [community group] is a bit social because I'm having that contact with people but not social in the sense of …*
Eden: *It's not your main social [outing]?*
Teresa: *No! … my finances and economics affect my ability to have a social life … [At an event we attended] I was going to talk about not having a social life and then I'm like "We aren't supposed to have a social life!"*

So, while alone, Teresa's income was primarily for buying food, and with this thriftiness was key. Thriftiness was a necessary skill to be stable on a fluctuating income. Teresa's background and teachings of her grandmother set her up to meet the challenges of getting by. Teresa took pride in this background and the skills of her family.

Teresa: *I've probably had this work ethic that came from my grandmother. She really [had] a sense of thriftiness. I had learnt from my grandmother, like how to save money you know having a bank account and having all that stuff. When I was [young] I worked, I made pocket money working on the farm in the summer holidays. So, I had a bank account and I had money in the bank account … because I was so good at saving money, my [Grandmother] taught me … and I had it hidden.*

Conversely, Teresa could not rely on her family for assistance. There were many long stories about these relationships, their economic and relational ups and downs, the disconnections, deaths, and the times they came together.

Teresa's thriftiness came to the forefront in her community group action: planning more food sharing. Unfortunately, members eager to help were often preoccupied with their own temporary employment and mutual obligations. The welfare system kept members focused on a worker–citizen lifestyle.

Teresa: *Yeah, but bloody [Mary] didn't bother telling anyone, I don't know if you heard but, she got a job! [Laughs] …*
Eden: *I wonder if it was like probably, I don't have a clue, or really know her.*
Teresa: *I don't know her that well either, I was a bit pissed off.*
Eden: *Did she feel it was like "Oh no, I shouldn't have got the job"?*
Teresa: *I know others would feel like that.*

There is a tension between social relationships and employment. Documenting movements away from common action through systemic and cultural forces towards work has a long academic tradition (Polanyi, 1944/2001; Simmel, 1908/1965). Solutions for the individual can be at detrimental to the group.

The other social connection and exchanges were Teresa's consistent dumpster diving or use of food banks to share food. Stigma associated with diving and food banks restrict these practices, and community members often avoided this association by avoiding the food.

Teresa: *… you need to be really sensitive about [different perspectives]. Like when we had that discussion, [Jill] was up there and we were talking about it. [We] were talking about having a food co-op and about food dumpster diving and [Bob] had said you couldn't have dived food available here, he was looking at like offering us a space there for a food co-op.*
Eden: *Is that a legal thing?*
Teresa: *No, it was a cultural, ethnic, thing. He said that there are some people, that come and use the service here, that it would be a real insult to them. Like ethnically type thing, and he said it would be a real slap in the face. He said it wouldn't matter how poor or desperate they were they wouldn't take it.*

While Teresa showed great respect for this pride, she reported disapproval that other community members, without the same contexts, still avoided taking cheap or free food.

[Talking about sharing dived food]
Teresa: *Yeah. I posted in the group, and I posted on my page I think one friend, I rang him … [to help him out] … which is the sort of stuff we need more of, of course.*
Eden: *The actual services [Foodbank] are not very friendly?*
Teresa: *Yeah, it's really hard to get fresh produce from the services like you can go in there and get a pack of pasta … can't even feed [it] to my [pets] [laughs]. I'm coming into contact with people that are low income I've got all this stuff it's really cheap, the people I thought*

> *would have wanted it aren't coming forward, and* ***it's like "How fucking desperate are you then?"***

In later conversations, Teresa explained how she filled medical prescriptions. After missing shifts she used a particular service for the medication where she herself avoided similar offers.

Eden: *You dropped shifts?*
Teresa: *Yeah.*
Eden: *You had to get medication from this place?*
Teresa: *I got a few scripts there.*
Eden: *There isn't much else to access is there?*
Teresa: *Not really. When I went to get help with the script the guy said "Oh, want some food?" I was like "No, I am right for food best not to take it" I said. I suppose it's not perishables, so I can just leave it in the cupboard, and it does help but I don't like to take stuff if I don't really need it. I prefer to leave it for people who really are in need. I went back and I needed [medication] that will cost me maybe only six dollars a time. But that is 18 or 20 dollars overall. I just cannot afford that.*

This is part of the big balancing act. People in poverty need to prove they are doing all they can to survive, that they do not need others help. This sometimes means rejecting help.

Similarly, Teresa had an old car, sitting out the front of her home. It let her get to work, it let her get to events, it let her get to food bank, but, of course, broke down. Money was needed to keep the car going, so Teresa reached out to financial services. Teresa was an avid saver but wanted to get the car inspected and repaired without losing her savings. To do so, she needed to reveal all her money activity to yet another stranger. Teresa was aggravated by this monitoring and the high effort needed to produce records. There was an implication of wrongdoing on her part throughout the experience.

Eden: *All that running around the punitive aspect of checking on you that you aren't horrible.*
Teresa: *Lying to them! Poor people lie!*

Teresa used her time as best she could. While she did not have a car, the bus allowed her the chance to collect cans for extra money as she came home from work shifts.

Teresa: *You collect the cans to get the money. And it's the way I see it, it's your money to do with as you wish. Like money from Centrelink is to do with as you wish.* ***But usually,*** *it is used for survival ... [so] if the bus takes its time, I go over the road and I just do this little circuit and collect some cans and bottles. And then it's quite funny on the bus because its packed. I was on the bus one night, it was so packed, and the way I was sitting, the bag fell over and all these bloody cans and bottles go rolling down the aisle and it [laughs]...*

Teresa also bought a new fridge and sardonically joked about how well it kept food.

Teresa: [Laughs] I was telling people about my new fridge, I said, I told people "Oh bloody hell it keeps food really long" I have things in there that are still okay a month later [laughs] I love my new fridge.

Financing that purchase required financial services. Teresa spent weeks investigating zero-interest loans, only to find using savings and the in-store repayments was a better option.

Teresa: My concern has been because I met with [financial services] last year a few of these people at a community meeting we had and I said "Just some feedback, my personal experience I would be better off going to [appliance stores] and getting one of their interest free terms like 5 years because I said going by your requirements, I could not afford to pay back a [zero interest] loan over the time period you offer".

Eden: Really? wow!

Teresa: Yep! On Newstart. So, it's just under 50 dollars a fortnight I know I can afford probably 25 a fortnight.

Teresa could afford these in-store repayments but only after the effort put in over weeks to investigate. Others will not have the time and energy to expend for comparing multiple loans and some may assume that zero-interest micro-financial solutions marketed to low-income earners are the best option.

Teresa was remarkably consistent on scoping out the best deals, often sharing where to get cheap fruit, vegetables, and, importantly for both of us, pet food. Despite savings from such deals, cost versus perishability was always an issue.

Teresa: This discussion online, the other day, about how fresh fruit is a luxury, and I said ***it is*** *a luxury for me! Like I will go to the market in town usually, I will buy the vegetables I need for meals, but I rarely buy fruit because by the time I buy the vegetables and everything for shopping I don't have anything left over for bananas. And then*

I have this thing about I don't use it and then it goes off ... I know it's something up here [points to head] like mentally that oh! I can't use it, or I can't wait ...

Teresa also spent time in markets. Finding the best discounts on necessities – often bought in bulk.

Teresa: *I was at the market; I'm trying to start up food sharing, and people can get everything they say is really hard work and this and that. So, I thought "Okay, I bought it, let's just see how interested people are" and I spent actually $20 of my money on all this produce, it was like a box of lettuce they are good quality, well by the end of the week they won't be [but] they are in the stay crisp bags.*

Markets, and auctions, required skills not needed in supermarkets. Teresa contrasted different levels of skills in the community.

Teresa: *[Sarah] came out to the market but she didn't come with me, we met each other there. I think it was the first experience because she was saying "Oh people are really pushy" and I said "Oh yeah! You have to stand your ground if there is something you want. You have to stand there, and people are very subtle, and they will really gently shove you out the way you have to stand your ground and shove back".*

Teresa gave other examples to show that a history of struggling was part of surviving well in poverty.

Teresa: *It's a shock to people when [they are well off and suddenly put in poverty]. Like I think of myself as like, um I've always ... not always but! ... I learnt my thriftiness from my grandmother and the fact I'm a tight arse Virgo, that's how I put it too [laughs]... I probably have a history of you know this, this is what we covered before, I've always had a history of probably working class from my grandparents.*

On these terms, Teresa directly reported no shame in using a food bank or dumpster diving, proudly describing the complexities of the practice as a skill and productive behaviour that not only fed her and her pets but also reduced waste in their community.

Teresa: *There is no shame in going to foodbank and I would want to share that ... there is no shame that we do this, it's not even just here for poor people it's here for everyone ... [On Dumpster Diving] it would make you cry when you see the waste that goes into those bins, and you know it's not "Ew, yuck" the food is actually quite good to take out of the bins; the bins are just a bit smelly, but the food is not badly affected by it.*

Teresa, extraordinarily confident and commanding, was still affected by others' stigmatising behaviour. One example occurred when merely trying to use a toilet at a food bank, which resulted in a threat to call the police.

Teresa: *You were talking about the "talk" [people must combat], it's like the experience I had at [foodbank] with the [worker] denying me access of the toilet!*

Eden: *With a sense of criminality?*

Teresa: ***Yeah, yeah!*** *I went to walk in and passed the other guy, that takes care of the cordial and cakes there, he put his hands out like this [over their front]! He was like "Oh we are not open yet! Not open yet!" I said, "I just wanted to-" and he just stepped out from his table, and someone brushed him with a stack of chairs, "can I just use the toilet, please?" and he said, "**See this is why we can't let people wander around its dangerous!**" ... I said "Please don't speak to me in that manner. I deserve to be treated with respect." That's how I said it. It's a bit of gaslighting and a bit of, this other guy stepped out and was like "You have been told we are not open, this is escalating, we are asking you to leave!" Like what the?! escalating which implied I raised my voice.*
*[Subsequent Conversation] ... So, it's a bit like when people have altercations with the police force, never having had a run in then one interaction and they are shocked by how they are treated, and **this is the real world**. Those that haven't utilised services or put up with that talk before have issues with that. But, you know, it's what I was saying previously too one of the workers at [financial services] and I got myself into trouble speaking up for myself. So, I just didn't access charity services when I needed them, and I was in a real pickle. Talking about 'the talk', the consequences of it!*

Teresa also took pride in avoiding luxury and unhealthy food, but the reality of what she could afford was often at odds with getting healthy food. Teresa still avoided talking about diving and haggling for food, but this was more about control over her identity.

Teresa: *I was telling them how I go dumpster diving, but I don't like to go in the local area, and they asked why that is, and I said "Oh". I really had to think about it afterwards because it was hard for me to explain what I was saying. It was in case I am recognised sort of. Like I think they were trying to work out why, given that I'm so open about it. I will talk about it to people, and sure I will talk to people at work, and I will let people know at work that I go dumpster diving. I had a think about it, and I emailed her, and I said "I have thought about it more and this probably explains it better. If someone from the local shops sees me … it's not me having the empowerment to tell them" … they may talk about oh that lady goes dumpster diving and then there are these judgements and stereotypes are created without them knowing who I actually really am.*

Feeling shame, for Teresa, was not the same as avoiding others negative stereotyping.

Many of our conversations took place in the public housing home Teresa lived in, at reduced rent but in very poor condition. Several times, during interviews, walking around the house and I put my hand to gaps in walls feeling the air outside. Teresa told me how weevils and moths get into the food. Poor housing was also about Teresa's health, she avoided colder, poorly seal, rooms in her own home and forgetting once to turn a heater off.

Teresa: *Four or five years ago I had a bill … Oh, [they were] ripping me off! A bill for 600 dollars but admittedly I had forgotten to turn the heater off a few nights.*

If you are not freezing at night in Australia, you are burning during the day:

Eden: *Do you have an AC?*
Teresa: *In the bedroom*
Eden: *Do you get to turn it on?*
Teresa: *If I can't sleep, then I will, I turn it on*
Eden: *That's an interesting thing sleep or the money?*
Teresa: *Yeah, it's easier to sleep during the day when it is hotter with a fan on me than at night. Even though it's cool outside, it's not cool inside.*

Teresa was, however, comfortable in her home, at least until the bureaucratic control moved from one organisation to another.

Teresa: *So, new financial shit!*
Eden: *So, this house is no longer under the government.*
Teresa: *… I went to pay rent at the new place last week and the guy came and said they were now [name]… [going into the new office] She was like we have 2 ways to pay rent centre-pay and that doesn't suit me cause my income is up and down. And then direct debit*

and I said that is not something I am doing that I am not giving my details of overdraft to an institution and then she snapped was like "You aren't going to pay rent then!". I'm so used to that attitude.

Worries over this treatment then impacted her family, as Teresa started to worry if pets would still be allowed. And again, she needed to provide all her banking details to another group of strangers to scrutinise. Similar poor treatment came from charity services when seeking assistance in her home.

Teresa: *I get this really insipid character come along with this manager, they made all these bloody assumptions, and the case worker, she could see I was stressed by having these two men in my house. These tall imposing men, making assumptions, you know like "Oh, so you fall asleep in your lounge quite a bit watching TV" and I was like "Why would you say that?" "Oh, because you have the blankets in here" … but other people, so what, if I fall asleep in front of the TV… I felt like saying "Why don't you understand how mental health effects people." I had bad experiences with charities being judged. So, again that links back into poverty when I go to get assistance from somewhere and being judged effects how you … So, yeah, I had been put off seeking any assistance!*

Teresa needed to maintain and find ways to reduce her reliance on, income, most notably because her resources were not only for herself but also for her pets. These pets represented an essential social relationship for Teresa, and the central capability of 'Other Species' "being able to live with concern for and in relation to animals, plants, and the world of nature" (Nussbaum, 2003, p. 42). That capability alone could be explored as it links with her childhood, her education, her previous work, hobbies, and passions but so could many of her other contexts. Still, this relationship with animals was not '*like* caring for dependents' but *was* caring for dependents. Her pets were family.

Teresa: *I spend like eighty dollars out of my dole check on my animals. Fifty to my vet each fortnight, for my never-ending vet bill, and I try to put thirty for pet food, but bloody pet food is going up, up, and up and the dole is not! It's getting really expensive to feed my dog, so yeah, if I say to someone how do you afford that? Yeah, it's like, well you don't have [pets]!*

Natalie

Natalie was a woman in her 30s, a part-time student, who was receiving Newstart payment, while attempting to move to the disability support pension. Natalie spoke directly on money, more than any other participant I interviewed. Economic issues intersected with disability making a good life seem further away. Natalie critiqued the welfare system and public were treating welfare recipients terribly, constantly questioning the authenticity and deservedness. The questioning increased when disability entered the picture. The political nature of the welfare bureaucracy was a spectre, waiting to take full control of through economics. This spectre took observable form as questioning frontline workers, dismissive owners of accommodation, and judgmental public fuelled by the misinformation of the media. Natalie's pathways speak to how money gives and takes control away (Figure 6.2).

Natalie did not elaborate on her childhood or history, but she did highlight generational and relational issues between herself and her family members because of the impositions of the welfare system.

Natalie: *It's sort of quite unnerving when you realise you are in a different class to your parents. Like my mother, she didn't have to, she grew up in massive poverty and stuff,* ***but now****. She is with her partner, and she doesn't have to worry about anything. When I talk to her about Centrelink, she doesn't have a clue because she was on a single parent payment like 20 years ago. So, when I say something about Centrelink, she says, "I know what it is like" and she doesn't know what it is like! I find it really insulting, they changed it massively, she didn't have to do obligations, she just got her money. She got cut off once, by an admin error, and had to go in before Christmas to be put back on which was stressful. She says "Oh, they treated*

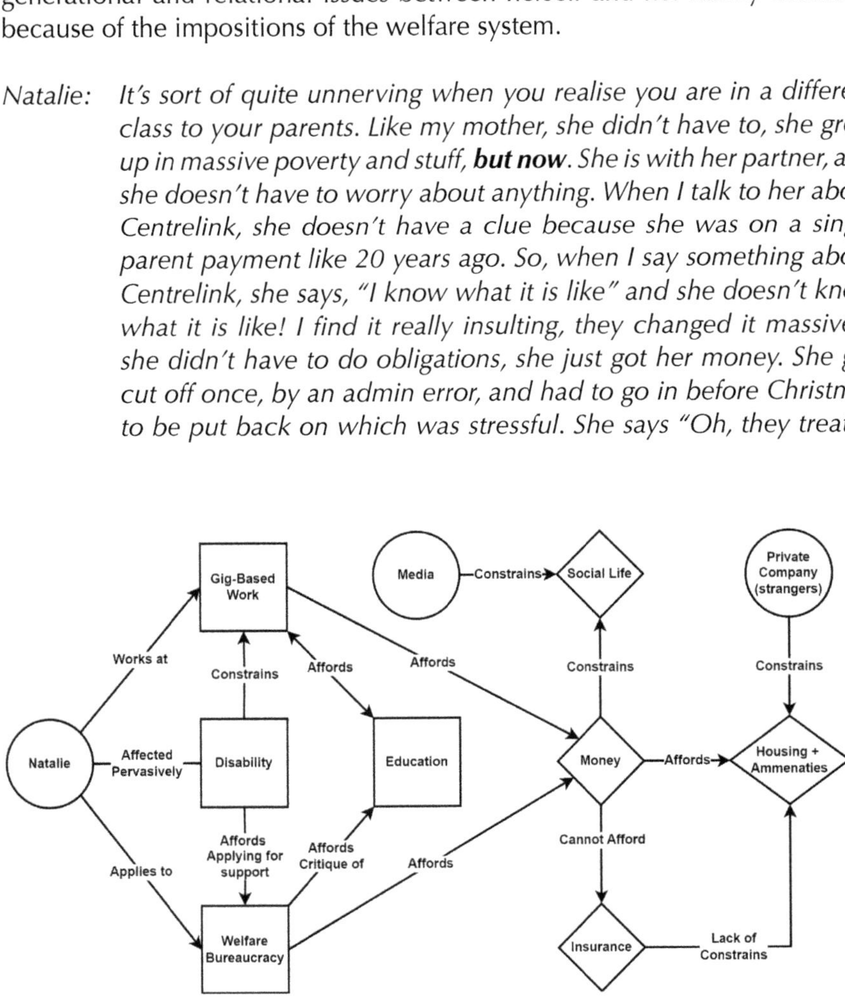

FIGURE 6.2 Natalie's pathways in poverty.

me terribly" which they do … But she doesn't know what it's like having the constant threat. I mean every appointment letter you get sent if you don't reply to it, you can be cut off.

Natalie balanced this conflict, and the issues in relating to her mother with a recognition of solidarity: living like that was still difficult. This sentiment was echoed by many group members – hard is hard, comparing trauma is not a solution to poverty.

Natalie: *There were times, like my mum was on single parent pension, well it wasn't, it was a single mother's pension. I remember she cried because she had run out of money, so she would then have to borrow money from me, from my piggy bank. She would cry as she was asking for it, because she felt so guilty, and she felt ashamed. She would pay me back! [She didn't get] child support back then, she didn't go for it, she didn't want to rock the boat … she would cry and there were times, but I mean I was always fed, she always, she worked very hard.*

Natalie said she could go to her mother for financial support but suggested it was too difficult. Obligations of reciprocity were avoided to avoid losing control.

The worry, pressure, and loss of control Natalie felt all only had the prospect of getting worse, more onerous, and more stigmatising.

Natalie: *Like all the things they are trying to do with all the welfare bills; the "three strikes and you are out". Because they are such horrible things. Like the drug testing and the welfare card, and they sneak this other stuff in, and it doesn't even get noticed. If that shit goes through my life will be infinitely worse. I was really upset when the government, this [conservative] government, got voted in because I knew my life would get worse and it has infinitely, **infinitely,** become worse already. They just do not care, and they think that I just don't deserve to live.*

The inevitability of obligations and sanctions generated most of Natalie's anxiety, especially being placed on a welfare card, removing her ability to decide where her money would be spent.

Eden: *[Robodebt] is a worry then?*
Natalie: *Yeah, yeah, for sure!*
Eden: *It's still a worry for you now? For a lot of people that saga, of Robodebt has ended, but for people like you, it hasn't?*

Natalie: *No, they are sending out more! I keep up with the news and I relentlessly read any welfare news because they keep trying to slide stuff in.* ***I am terrified of being put on a cashless welfare card*** *and I get sick of going online and seeing all these people go "Oh well, they should just be happy they get anything at all!" and "At least they shouldn't be spending it on drugs and alcohol!" or "Oh it won't affect you if you aren't doing the wrong thing". I do not want to be on a cashless welfare card! I manage my money and I would find it really demeaning like I'm, how old am I? I am [30+] years old,* ***I know how to manage.***

Natalie had been assessed for limitations to work, and this led to limited job-seeking obligations which reduced pressure, but recent changes in policy turned the relaxation into anxiety.

Natalie: *It fulfilled my obligations, then when they bring the new legislation in it didn't count. I got told, and then they put me in with the disability employment service. When they reassessed me, and I was told by the worker that they would be "much more accommodating of my barriers" and that was like the biggest load of bullshit! I have ever [laughs] … I don't know if they actually believed it or not! They seemed to believe it. But it is just not. My life has just been … I don't know if I should say hell, but it has just been relentlessly horrible ever since [laughs]*

Many people in the group took tiny windows of reprieve from the system. Discussions at events were about how to get doctors' notes as evidence of illness as the only sure way to gain temporary exemption. A break was needed, and generally positive, but knowing you will re-enter the system again was just as worrying as the system itself.

Natalie: *… basically I have been in the system for a while and the obligations are probably the thing that causes me the most mental anguish, the most stress! It's probably the thing that effects my mental health the most. If they would just leave me alone that would make me really happy! I am doing everything I am physically capable of. It has been acknowledged that I have barriers to working full time and they just … The amount of time that they have breached protocols and yeah, the disability employment networks* ***are not*** *more considerate! They are not trained in anything … At the moment I have an exemption because I'm on a sick certificate.* ***Thank God!*** *But that only lasts until [next month] so I am actually dreading it* *being stopped. I get a bit of a break and then I think I can breathe again, but the time is coming up and it's freaking me out.*

Natalie churned in poverty for a long time, on and off Newstart for over ten years. She had limited job opportunities, had poor mental health, and developed a physical disability. Like many poor people, her previous employment was now impossible due to disability. Natalie experienced the full range of government-imposed obligations and directed her efforts to learning as much as she could about these systems to better churn.

Natalie: *I've been on Newstart, on and off, since I came back from overseas, I was [in my 20s]. I'm [in my 30s] now. So, in between that time I have had paid work! I have had a few different jobs. I came back from overseas, and I went on [welfare] and it was very different then to what it is now, in terms of obligations, and how my life is now compared to 10 years ago! So, the obligations and stuff are the things that put the most stress on my life … that is what puts the most impact on me! It doesn't help me find a job, it doesn't motivate me, it doesn't do any of the things that the government claims that it does!*

Natalie was active in the community group which afforded some opportunities for work. 'Who you know', networking, was necessary for work opportunities. Agitation is luckily largely free.

Natalie: *One good thing about activism is it gives opportunities that I wouldn't otherwise have. For instance, I won't say the name, I found out through a protest, [someone] told me about an opportunity for [work], and I put my work in, and they said it's quite good and I should be paid for it by the end of the month … What happened was after that then I had to do media for [welfare advocacy]* ***because****, one of the problems is when you are in activism. Like what happens when you are poorer is, anytime anyone needs like a poor soundbite they ask you … So, we do all this content, and giving them all this, these people for their media stories, and we get absolutely nothing in return. [One group] are pretty good, they will sometimes … last time they did one with me, a media release, I did get a little bit of an honorarium for my time.*

I witnessed several cases of working opportunities through the community group. They were always short term, precarious jobs that allowed stability as churning in poverty. Often the jobs were directly about combatting poverty with others; what could be considered a positive function of poverty (see Gans, 1972). Something this very chapter could be considered.

Natalie was passionate about her career path; she was able to secure some one-off jobs. These gigs came with anxiety over how the extra money fit into welfare payments, and bureaucratic monitoring and judgement. The other option is to take work, but not take money.

Eden: *That is your profession now, isn't it? That is what you are doing?*
Natalie: *I'm not getting paid.*
Eden: *That is the thing, is it a profession if you aren't paid?*
Natalie: *Is it a profession or is it a labour of love? Where I get no money and I do a lot of unpaid work? And that is what I am realising because I have done a lot of unpaid work for activism, but the main reason you do it is because you* ***think*** *work is important but if it means being disrespected and your experience isn't being seen as a positive and you just can't stand the people that you are working with. I don't know what to do.*

The interaction between mental health and disability was stark through the group and beyond – Natalie's experience was no exception.

Natalie: *I came back from overseas; I was on Newstart, I did a course; [a certificate], and I worked in [the area]. I was a receptionist for a while and then because of certain mental health things, the job would not give me time off to go to a support group that I wanted to go to, so I had to [skip work], they fired me.*

For Natalie, the system of social security was one of denigration and mistrust. She had been badgered by frontline workers questioning the legitimacy of her disability claims. These experiences were at the centre of mounting anxiety for the future. Natalie would not let these people stop her pursuing her goals despite the worry they caused.

Natalie: *I've left multiple appointments at [job provider] in tears when I was quizzed by one worker. They asked me "What is the point of you studying?" They were just like the first worker I had there, and at first, they seemed quite consolatory.*
Eden: *Like he was trying to be friendly to you?*
Natalie: *Yeah, but it didn't last long. Then there was one appointment where they were like "So, you are studying? So, you are studying [field]. Well! You know what are you going to do with that!? There are not many jobs in [that area]"*
Eden: *Yeah, that interrogating of choices?*

Natalie: ***Yes!*** *Interrogating my life choices and then they go "Well …" because I said, "Look I am going to apply for the DSP" but then they go "Well if you are applying for the DSP, what is the point of you studying?!" and I was like … "what do you mean?" And he was like well "What's the point if you are not going to, if you feel like you can't work, and you are not capable for work, what is the point of your studying?" and I had to sit there and try to justify … Anytime you go there your every life choice is scrutinised … I left that appointment feeling absolutely horrible, because I think I guess I shouldn't study then. What is the point? I felt really hopeless, and I thought "well you know [the worker] is saying what is the point, maybe, what is the point?" and I was … it really made me want to quit, to be honest, it made me want to quit my studies.*

Applications to Disability Support Pensions (DSP) were common in the group. Unfortunately, the most common reason to be rejected was being assessed "across too many tables". If someone suffered from multiple issues, each was considered separately, for example, separating mental illness and physical disability and individual body parts are singled out rather than considered together as a diagnosis. Without one single compromised part of their body or mind on the assessment tables, group members rarely would qualify for DSP. You could try again with different medical support letters, which attempted to speak to the truth of their experience, but these were often repeated attempts.

Natalie: *They don't like giving exemptions. If it's something permanent, then you should be on the DSP. So, then you apply for it, but you still don't get it …*
Eden: *… one thing I have got from all the interviews is not to trust the job network or even Disability Employment Services [DES]*
Natalie: ***Don't trust them!*** *DES are really, my friend is on the DSP, and she can't work, she applied 3 times, and she finally got it.*
Eden: *You applied in the end?*
Natalie: *I applied, and I was rejected …*
Eden: *… Was it because you don't have enough points in any of those categories?*
Natalie: *Yeah! So, they are like "Oh, sorry"*

Like other group members, and other interview participants, Natalie's experiences with mental health and support services were marred by a distinct lack of understanding and relationship building.

Eden: *Unfortunately, everyone's responses have been that they are not very helpful I was wondering your take on that interaction?*

Natalie: *On mental health services*
Eden: *Especially if it intersects with your poverty which it does mainly, I guess*
Natalie: *Yes! I mean my mental health would be like 1000 times better if I didn't have to deal with the bullshit of the disability employment service. If I wasn't constantly in fear of being cut off my payment.*

Natalie was judged and controlled by people outside her immediate social relationships including media and strangers – including landlords. Natalie spent most of her money on her small unit. Not only rent, but electricity bills she could not explain, damages due to flooding with no insurance, and most of all, the loss of communal washing machines that forced her to wash clothes by hand, aggravating her medical conditions.

Natalie: *[Doing laundry] is not good for my hands, [because of my illness]. It effects my hands the worst but yeah … I that is why I couldn't do [work] full time.*

Furthermore, a stranger crashed into her car, and while it was still drivable, the costs of repairs were more than the car and the payout was not enough for a new vehicle – a catch-22. For all these cases, Natalie spoke with a sense of angry sadness at the lack of any real opportunity for control, due to so many of the people involved in these incidents being strangers, sometimes ghost like due to the automation.

Natalie: *Yeah [my electricity bill] was $500. And I live by myself in a bedsit, so I am not very happy with my living situation at the moment.*
Eden: *500 dollars for a bedsit!?*
Natalie: *Yeah, it's not great I don't have gas cooking … It's a bedsit. At the moment I'm having issues because I am in a block of units … but they had a communal laundry, part of the reason I moved in was like "Okay it's pretty shitty, but at least I don't have to pay for my laundry" … The place before I had to leave, because my flat flooded. I just came home to water pouring out of the ceiling lights the tenant upstairs left their tap on … [my] stuff was ruined … I had no contents insurance because-*
Eden: *You couldn't afford it?*
Natalie: ***Couldn't afford it** and needed $30,000 of stuff to insure and people were like why didn't you have content insurance?*
Eden: *And then it was your fault that someone else flooded your unit?*
Natalie: *Yeah, yeah, yeah basically, yeah! So, it just permeates just every facet of your life not having enough money!*

Big issues were caused by acts of strangers. Small mercies like the communal washing were in the control of these strangers.

Natalie: *"Why remove the 3 washing machines why not leave them?" and [accommodation representative] is like "Oh, I think did that as a courtesy with housing manager"!* ***Imagine someone*** *taking or stealing your washing machine!* ***Imagine****! I don't really use that machine, but* ***you just don't have control over your life****. And they put in this letter, the audacity to say that the laundromat is nearest is on the opposite side of the suburb! Four kilometres away! So, if you don't drive … They haven't said they will reduce the rent or anything like that in relation to that legally … but I'm on a periodic lease as well, so there is a danger, because I want to complain in writing but if I do, they may kick me out!*

While she had to keep silent at times, Natalie was still a vocal activist. At the same time, she was hesitant to speak about her past. She spoke of losing friends when she was vocal. Those friends, learning from media, argued Natalie was not *really* poor; at least when compared to developing economies. Natalie fought against being seen as 'not poor enough' to talk with any authority on hardship.

Natalie: *I want to preface this, I know you probably get heaps of things, like whenever, I am hesitant to even talk about this kind of stuff. Whenever you do it online or you say it, you have people that are like "You should be grateful that you live in a country that does give welfare". I have got into it with friends because they say go to a third world country and you can like you know have sex with old men for money because they, it's just, it's impossible. I'm not really friends with them anymore … There were these posters everywhere at uni [about eating on a dollar a day] and I wrote on social media "I'm getting really sick of this like live below the line campaign I don't need to be told how to live below the line I'm doing it! I'm eating noodles every day, I don't need, like it's not a novelty."*

Media teaches that poverty is absolute, is death and destitution, is forced sex work, murder, or starvation, and in turn this limited the legitimacy of Australians to claim they experienced poverty as well as making jobs like sex work seem like immoral suffering along with starvation and destitution. This may be a key reason why focusing on one indicator as 'poverty' was avoided – these poor people were sick of having their suffering questioned or delegitimised, or worse played up as a game; for example, CEO sleepouts were heavily criticised by the community.

Economic issues harmed interpersonal relationships. Natalie worried about giving gifts. She worried about spending time with others. She limited social participation. Natalie did her best to work through these constraints but was constantly aware that being seen as frivolous was confirmation to others that she was not 'really' poor.

Natalie: *It's not nice that you feel like you can't be generous with other people, or just easier, to offer to buy them you know drinks or shout them. It doesn't make you feel good. It's nice like if someone were to do that and I do that sometimes.*

Eden: *You find that it all limits when you can go out with people?*

Natalie: *Yeah! And the type of present that I want to buy them in terms of no one goes "Oh, what a shitty present".*

Eden: *But you know, you know that?*

Natalie: *You can't spend the same amount on them as they would on you which makes you feel bad.*

Gifts to others was not the only worry. Gifts to herself were hedonistic – the quick intuitive system seeking gratification, 'just treat yourself'. I know forgoing your birthday is not a real suggestion of cognitive theories, but forgoing these behaviours is how that double thinking trickles into behaviour of poor and non-poor people.

Natalie: *I also think, because I'm friends with a lot of people that are poor, I can't just have my birthday. I'm having my birthday this Friday and I want to go to the [venue]. Something is on, and it is 15 dollars. But I don't want to force people to spend money. Actually, when I was trying to choose where to go, to eat, there was a restaurant I was trying to book and they had a minimum spend of 25 per person … which I really disagree with on principle because some people, I have been in that position before, where you gone out and you are in a big group and you only have like 10 or 15 dollars to spend. You still want to go and be sociable and stuff … I don't like* ***forcing*** *people to spend money and I was quite incensed at that! I changed the restaurant based on that because that really pissed me off, and I think it's* ***really rude*** *and elitist!*

Again, like everyone I spoke to, Natalie was not someone who *really* needed assistance, she managed her finances well. That managing like others meant she went without some needs.

Natalie: *I take pride in being able to feed myself. When I dumpster dive, I go with a friend and she knows people that really rely on it in the*

> *group, on social media. Stuff where people, if they get excess of something, they give it away. I'm not gonna, it seems like if people think that you have enough food then you are* ***not really*** *poor. So, that really Dickensian thing. It's hard to explain to people who are not in poverty.* ***I have to because I don't really think about it, this is just my life****!*

Altogether, almost everything in Natalie's pathways constrained her personal control over her environment and her daily life. Even without directly stating her stress and worry, this loss of control produced the multiple overlapping health, mental, social, and economic constraints which provide a picture of a life that deserves more freedom – unfortunately policy changes to welfare provision since our conversations make Natalie's worst nightmares more likely.

Conclusion

I do not want to construct something here. I do not want to tell you what is important in these stories. You should take away what you can learn about the experience of poverty you can. I think these stories, as broken up and shrunk as they are, stand as obvious evidence to our needs to rethink poverty, to rethink policy, and to rethink how we approach learning what is best for any individual. I hope that the summary of experiences and these two cases show you the patterns, pathways, and problems you can look for in your clinical settings, in your research, and in your everyday interactions with people getting by.

References

Crowe, D. (2020). Labor steps up push for more aid for workers, unemployed. *The Sydney Morning Herald*. www.smh.com.au/politics/federal/labor-steps-up-push-for-more-aid-for-workers-unemployed-20200518-p54u1t.html?utm_medium=Social&utm_source=Twitter

Davidson, P., Saunders, P., Bradbury, B., & Wong, M. (2020). Poverty in Australia 2020: Part 1, overview. ACOSS/UNSW Poverty and Inequality Partnership Report No. 3. ACOSS.

Department of Social Services (DSS). (2018). *DSS payment demographic data*. https://data.gov.au/data/dataset/cff2ae8a-55e4-47db-a66d-e177fe0ac6a0

Duke, J. (2020). 10 Coalition MPs back cut to JobSeeker supplement, but majority rule out snap back to $40 a day. *The Sydney Morning Herald*. www.smh.com.au/politics/federal/10-coalition-mps-back-cut-to-jobseeker-supplement-but-majority-rule-out-snap-back-to-40-a-day-20201024-p5685v.html

Gans, H. J. (1972). The positive functions of poverty. *American Journal of Sociology*, *78*(2), 275–289. https://doi.org/10.1086/225324

Nussbaum, M. (2003). Capabilities as fundamental entitlements: Sen and social justice. *Feminist Economics, 9*(2–3), 33–59. https://doi.org/10.1080/1354570022000077926

Polanyi, K. (1944/2001). *The great transformation: The political and economic origins of our time*. Beacon press.

Simmel, G. (1908/1965). The poor (C. Jacobson, Trans.). *Social Problems, 13*(2), 118–140.

Thain, A. (2020). *Rethinking poverty: A qualitative study of becoming resource and relationship constrained in South Australia*. Unpublished PhD Thesis. University of South Australia. https://hdl.handle.net/11541.2/144892

Whiteford, P. (2016). Election FactCheck Q&A: Is it true Australia's unemployment payment level hasn't increased in over 20 years? *The Conversation*. https://theconversation.com/election-factcheck-qanda-is-it-true-australias-unemployment-payment-level-hasnt-increased-in-over-20-years-59250

7

DISCOURSES IN POVERTY

Throughout the previous chapters, I commented on what happened but also *how people spoke about their experiences*. In a non-cognitivist perspective, verbal reports are their own thing, and not direct reports of internal psychological experience (Guerin, 2016; Guerin et al., 2018). Participants' talk is not evidence of internal, personal aspirations, but a functional tool in context. Language use does not simply describe reality but rather *does something* to audiences. For that reason, I want to take a step away from describing the narratives as 'what happened' and discuss how different groups speak about poverty. This is important because you will probably talk with poor people more than you participate and observe their everyday life.

I have not completed an analysis à la Potter and Wetherell (1987) or Critical Discourse Analysis (Fairclough, 2004). Instead, I focus on the function of discourse in context (Guerin, 2016). The poor are not a hermetically sealed, excluded group, but rather a group that must constantly interact and strive to be included and to do so they must skilfully use discourse to achieve different outcomes with different audiences. There is no separation between the material reality of poverty and how those in poverty talk through their experience. As Phelan (2014, pp. 34–36) argues, we need to understand discursive practice as wholistic, or a "structural totality", intertwined with the materiality of the situation. How people talk is how they get their resources, manage their relationships and 'get by'.

Analysing the Discourses of the 'Poor'

How people speak about issues is just as important as the experiences. Analyses of discourse include both participants' and others (media and

DOI: 10.4324/9781003453970-7

politicians') discourses. Two findings arose in the literature: neoliberalism and the phantom poor.

Neoliberal Discourses

As the zeitgeist of our time, neoliberalism is promoting self-determination through absolute self-responsibility, as independent actors interacting with 'the market'. This individual focus is why victim-blaming survives despite challenges, caveats, and careful wording. Examples in the literature included: self-responsibility for obesity implying poor people have limited knowledge, or intelligence, for healthy eating (Farrel et al., 2016, p. 3); or mothers blamed for not taking on worker identities (Pulkingham et al., 2010).

Verdouw (2017) is the clearest exploration of on-the-ground neoliberalism. Middle class and working-class people were agreeing with neoliberal tenets while those that rejected them were those with the economic resources to exit the rat race. Many other texts included some comment on neoliberalism both socially and through policy (Cook, 2012; Shildrick & Macdonald, 2013; Jette & Rail, 2014, pp. 207, 209; Garthwaite, 2015, p. 43; Strier et al., 2016; Stahl & Habib, 2017; Ali et al., 2018). Research however focuses on "broad brushstrokes" of neoliberalism rather than the individual effects (Verdouw, 2017, p. 525). Separating neoliberalism as ideology, discourse, or practical implications for everyday behaviour is artificial, it all happens together.

Participants often endorsed, agreed with, or used *dominant discourses and ideological positions* comparing their life to other poor people. Such participants blamed the poor using the constructs of poor choices, or poor work ethic. Many agreed with the dominant discursive patterns of neoliberalism including: that the individual is responsible for their poverty (Broughton, 2003; Reid & Tom, 2006; Marston, 2008; Pulkingham et al., 2010; Chaufan et al., 2013), that a meritocracy is effective (Godfrey & Wolf, 2016; Ali et al., 2018), that a 'just world' exists (Godfrey & Wolf, 2016; Verdouw, 2017), and that the poor need more assistance to correct their thinking and behaviour (Mason et al., 2014). Other agreements, reported in previous chapters as harmful, arose such as claims poverty only exists in the 'developing world' (Shildrick & MacDonald, 2013). Those ways of talking – therefore thinking (Guerin, 2016) – open the doors for infantilising, dehumanising, and often punitive approaches to reduce poverty (e.g., Broughton, 2003).

The Phantom Poor – Blaming Other Poor People

All these agreements interacted with 'othering': poor people constructing a phantom group of 'other poor people'. Participants were not those that needed assistance, but there were poor people in need of assistance and correction (Ali et al. 2018; Broughton, 2003; Patrick, 2016; Shildrick

& Macdonald, 2013). Once referred to as the "attributional paradox" (Broughton, 2003, p. 47). That paradox occurs while sometimes rejecting the identity of 'poor' altogether or taking that identity on only as structural truth rather than personal identity (Broughton, 2003; Godfrey & Wolf, 2016; cf. Townsend, 1979).

That *other* group of poor people were the ones avoiding work, taking drugs, parenting without work, or choosing welfare. This group were to blame for both their poverty and the stigmatised image placed on other poor people. Shildrick and MacDonald noted that studies do not find anyone who was part of this 'phantom' category, nor did participants give explicit examples that were checkable (MacDonald & Marsh, 2005, cited in Shildrick & MacDonald, 2013, p. 291). The construction of this group *functioned to building the speaker as a moral and deserving poor person*, while denigrating and blaming this phantom, and maybe fictitious, undeserving group of poor people for stigma and policies that harmed them.

Australian-Specific Discourses

Maybe most common is the construction of 'dole bludgers' – a derogatory term for recipients implying they are willing to be on *the dole* (Marston, 2008). 'Dole bludger' is an Australian variety of 'welfare chiseller', 'welfare queen', or 'scrounger' (Dodson, 2013; Patrick, 2016). The *dole bludger construct* frames taxpayers as victims of economic issues while also delegitimising claims that the system is unjust for welfare recipients (Archer, 2006, 2009).

Australians in poverty use this construct; some people are dole bludgers, but at the same time there are not enough jobs (Grahame & Marston, 2012). Peel (2003, pp. 31, 111) spoke of self-deprecating uses when hope for employment was lost. In welfare reform literature, the issue of 'bludger' versus the 'taxpayer' or 'Aussie battler' appears (Baum & Duvnjak, 2013, p. 14; Deeming & Smyth, 2015, p. 315; Engels, 2006, p. 6; Marston & Macdonald, 2007, p. 235). Dichotomising of deservedness is key to limiting change in society – "we will not raise incomes of a bludger at the expense of a battler".

Another categorical label has arisen: 'Job Snob'. Low job availability and quality leads to people seeming picky about the work they take (Peel, 2003, p. 181; Marston, 2008, pp. 365–367). The implication is a snobbish attitude, laced with hedonism, delusions of high status, or arrogance are the true causes of unemployment, simultaneously delegitimising claims that poor-quality jobs are harmful or unjust. Former Prime Minister Tony Abbott implied young job seekers are "too fussy" and were "only working on their own terms", but when asking young job seekers to reflect on these statements, they reframed their choices as resistance against poor working conditions or menial labour (Marston, 2008, pp. 367–368). Or participants argued the need of fussiness as a balance against demands of care work (Broughton, 2003).

Seemingly in response, work-first welfare policy can de-gender mothers to promote a worker identity (Gazso, 2007). Frontline workers similarly use a moral underclass discourse, suggesting welfare recipients were 'unable' to understand or incorrectly assess outcomes of employment (Arthurson & Jacobs, 2009, pp. 186–187; Pulkingham et al., 2010; also see Levitas, 2005). Again, like in psychology literature, poor mental skills or abilities are constructed with dispositional fault being the cause of poverty.

Why Go Along with These Discourses

Often more research is called for, otherwise, researchers suggest their participants' beliefs were either 'critical' or not, or that data indicates the mainstream values were 'held' and 'acted on' (Marston, 2008, p. 359; Woodward, 2008, p. 164). But just because people say something does not mean they 'hold' those beliefs and values, and it is more likely participants hold *various and contradictory* ways of talking depending on the context (Guerin, 2016; Guerin & Wood, 2017; Harper, 1996). If saying something made it my core beliefs and values I would exercise more, eat better, and sleep better. Potentially the form or context of research makes expressing one view more likely than others.

In another case, agreement with neoliberal discourses and the 'othering' of the phantom wrongdoing poor group are said to be "driven by deep-seated psychological needs to (consciously and unconsciously) justify the system" (Godfrey & Wolf, 2016, p. 101). The issue here is making a generalised claim well beyond the scope of the data relying on a psychological reduction. Turning complex phenomenon into some internal unobserved inner aspect is a weak but constant psychological trope that should be avoided.

If those conclusions are compared to more contextualised findings, more variations appear. For example, Broughton (2003, pp. 48–49) found participants in a work programme agreed with the infantilising and blaming discourses produced by the programme facilitators – even reproducing them – but they did so because resistance could lead to removal from the programme and stopping of welfare payments. When that possibility was removed – after participants graduated the programme – participants then reproduced the previously found 'phantom group' discourse that they were not the target audience, but 'others' were. This is evidence that the concrete documentable functions for discursive behaviour change with the contexts in which they appear and is why pairing context and discourse is essential.

Authors suggested we need 'better' or 'good' images and discourses of poverty and unemployment (Palmer et al., 2004; Marston, 2008; Farrell et al., 2016; Gibson, 2011; Pemberton et al., 2016; Shildrick & Macdonald, 2013). Others suggested the need for more 'solidarity' between the working class and the poor (Gibson, 2011; Shildrick & MacDonald 2013), and the need for academics and the poor to actively combat dominant discourses (Pemberton et al., 2016). I only had more questions: Does the mere presence of better or realistic discourses or images of the poor mean they will be used? If there are 'good' images or discourse, what contexts allow, or hinder, their use in everyday life and in the media? A contextual analysis would suggest the mere presence of opposing discourses is not enough, rather function – what do those ways of talking get us – are important.

The discourses that follow people in poverty through everyday life are harmful, infantilising and stigmatising. Through media, and in everyday interactions with friends and frontline workers poor people are blamed and put down. I would argue that experiencing this denigration is a key stressor and is part of the cognitive feedback loop, further restricting people's ability to get out of poverty. Otherwise, we need more knowledge on the *function* of discourses in everyday contexts. So, rather than just asking poor people to talk, we need to directly observe in what contexts they use these ideas.

Discourses in My Data

In most adult human social interactions, talking is the primary form of 'getting stuff done' (Guerin, 2015, 2016, 2017). Most of what the participants did with each other was talking, most of the positive attempts to better their position in society involved trying to change how they or others spoke about the poor, and most of the negative experiences from others came in the form of something said. All that talk directly changed the available resources and social relationships. The issue is many cases of those saying impactful things were impactful not because they were true, right, good, or kind, but because that person was in control of resources.

One finding stood out against the call for better images. It seemed, early in the research, that the very nature of striving for a better image or identity for the poor has recursive effects on poverty. Trying to be 'better' often meant saying you survive alone and are an effortful hard worker. As the participants, and the group, tried to present themselves in a better light they often reinforce not only the stereotypes of the poor but then acted in line with that discourse, ultimately denying help.

That presentation of the self is for others, it is to manage image, to manage relationships and, therefore, manage resources. In *The purchase of intimacy*, Zelizer describes how discursive practice relates to everyday relational work: "people erect a boundary [but also] mark the boundary by means of names and practices [and] establish a set of distinctive understandings and practices that operate within that boundary …" (2010, p. 35; also Bandelj, 2012, p. 182). The boundaries for the poor are predetermined by others, including the media and policy. The participants knew simply talking would not directly change the boundaries but talking was an attempt to reconstitute their social identity as someone deserving, not 'that type of poor person'. In these boundaries, the expectations of worker citizenry are set and spoken.

Teresa: *That is what I was saying last year at [an event] the shit that people say ... [laughs] that is so fucking easy isnt it ... Oh yeah, like start a business, or start work rurally, or something I don't want to have to do.*

The fight was between having rights as a person and being a good worker. Work is the hurdle, the obligation, to deserve assistance. Many scholars have argued this is illogical; you cannot expect those with nothing to then give to society (Coser, 1965; Mazelis, 2017; Simmel, 1908/1965). The argument continues in policy; we avoid life-first welfare provision aimed at mental and social health and champion obligation-based work-first models with punishment and control (Brown et al., 2017). These systems are the stress faced by poor people in Australia.

The verbal tools for relating to others include the categories of wrongdoer, bludger, or cheat. The psychological reduction would say using these against others is simply "internalisation of public sentiment" or there are simply no other repertoires to draw on. Instead, I argue, these participants, and the group, were constantly balancing between the dominant notions of the worker-citizen, or neoliberal discourses, and their solidarity. Figure 7.1 sets out the discourses, their repertoires, the contexts I recorded in my research as influencing them. The conflict between the two main discourses, *Neoliberal* and *Solidarity*, creates a balancing act. Each source or discourse controls resources and relationships – money, education opportunities, employment.

Repertoires are the collection of constructs, metaphors, phrases, figures of speech, or stories that make up the discourse. Repertoires can be implemented functionally to work with, work against, or even generate new discourses (Dean, 2003, p. 5; Parker, 2002; Potter & Wetherell, 1987). The community group members used these ways of talking but that does not suggest they believe in what is said. Rather, these repertoires are functional in context, talking with others to maintain exchanges and get by. Using a repertoire is not a choice but rather a means to livelihood, relationships, and identity. The same phrases, metaphors, and figures can be said in different contexts to different effects (Dean, 2003; Harper 1996).

Neoliberal Discourses

Participants were proud of their self-reliance, self-help, and personal responsibility, reproducing 'Neoliberal Discourses'. Parallels between these instances of talk and wider examinations of neoliberal discourse were

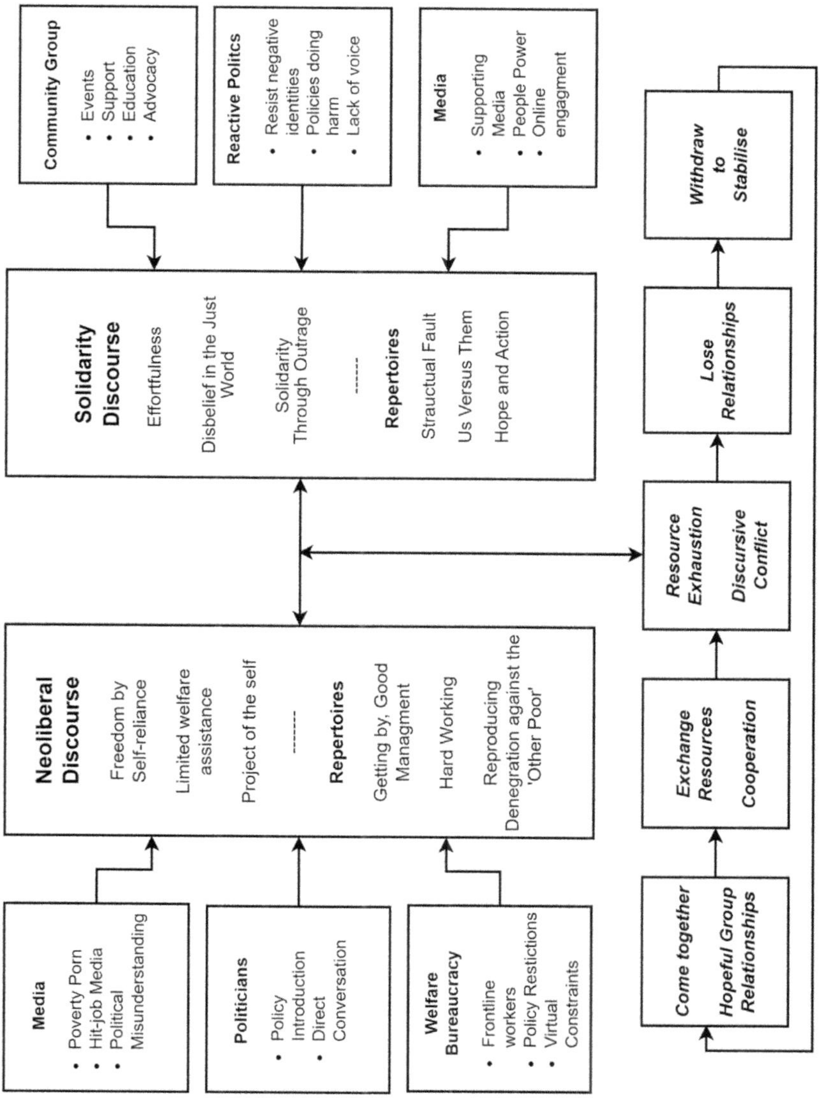

FIGURE 7.1 Neoliberal and solidarity discourses and the balancing act.

clear – and are widespread (Fairclough, 2002; Springer, 2012). The use of these was not clear-cut agreement, but rather a constant negotiation.

Media

Before, during, and after my PhD I have documented consistent problematic and harmful portrayals of the poor, welfare recipients, and the unemployed. From news and social media, the portrayals are circulated around and around. Participants often commented on or discussed these, for example for Adam a particular news cycle took aim at community groups and labelled them "dole bludgers clubs". Adam separated the criticism from himself – he was not a dole bludger – but spoke to the emotive and social effects that the news had. Natalie collided with media portrayals of poverty as eating only rice; the false binary that she must not be poor because she spends more than a dollar a day on food. Challenging these can be harmful, as challenge suggests you are 'that poor person'. Be it communal or personal, the effects of the Australian media's individualisation of poverty have wide-reaching effects.

Policy

Welfare provision in Australia often questions the 'genuine' need for assistance of the poor. These come from the residual nature and means-testing of the system and constant political discourse that welfare recipients should not complain: "it could be worse", "there are plenty of opportunities". At the same time, participants constantly worried about policy – cashless welfare cards, Robodebt, and new obligations, always framed as 'helping' when the group and participants knew it would only hurt.

The issue was more direct when engaging politicians. I was present for discussion with local government councillors and state and federal politicians; they simply questioned the very nature of poverty. In private meetings they hedged their claims "I know this isn't what you want to hear", in public they were overt and aggressive "what you people need to learn is ...", and in official statements presenting the position a party or governing body they spoke down to the group members as parents caring for a wayward child. Others voiced sympathetic messages, some supported calls for a raise to NewStart, but equally conservative politicians stood up to tell group members they had not done enough for themselves, often suggesting getting loans to start businesses, to take one of the "many jobs on offer", suggesting as business owners they "never get applicants". Otherwise, they admonished the group trying to edify them on welfare provision, "These are for basic support and not lives of luxury".

Welfare Bureaucracy

Frontline workers and service providers directly interrogate the efforts, plans, and the identity of the poor. Paternalism and infantilisation were strong features in the stories of participants. These tendencies are aligned with the tenants of the neoliberal progression in welfare policy (Marston, 2008, p. 362). Frontline workers reproduced self-reliance and independent responsibility talking points. Sandra, Emily, and Natalie as people experiencing disability were challenged to forgo study. For Adam, frontline workers 'educated' him to announce and admit any wrongdoing but could not expect workers to admit their erroneously applied breaches, cutting off his payment. The issue, and the solutions, were squarely placed on the effortfulness of the poor (Gibson, 2009). The solution was never on the bureaucratic side of the exchange.

Community group members were given wrongdoer identities, Teresa being treated as a criminal by volunteers in charities when attempting to use the toilet, or house assistance services implying disorganisation was rooted in laziness. Politicians implied the groups were trying to take what was not deserved. And the media fearmongered that they were just criminals. Unfortunately, these aspects were also reproduced by participants and group members, often suggesting laziness when others could not complete jobs, or suggesting that some members' use of drugs and alcohol produced their poverty. In these reproductions, there was always the intent to convey that they, as an individual, were not part of this group of those responsible for their poverty; to maintain their deservedness and survive poverty, they could not be "that poor person" (also see Mazelis, 2015, 2017).

Repertoires of Neoliberalism

There are three major groupings of interpretive repertoires. Table 7.1 sets out some of the observed elements involved in each which informed the neoliberal, self-reliant, claims and comments of participants.

These ways of talking are resistance to the assumptions of the *dole bludger, job snob*, and *essentialist (lazy)* categorisation of poor people. By insisting on their independence and self-reliance with a small pool of resources, participants are rejecting failure or a lack of effort. By doing so, however, neoliberal values and beliefs are promoted. I found most of this talk was directed at those who might be considered 'outside' the community and impossible to get 'onside' with solidarity discourse.

Powerful strangers could, however, use these ways of talking against the group. Many of the claims in these repertoires, if treated as absolute truth, would be justification to remove assistance. If welfare recipients are doing so

TABLE 7.1 Repertoires of the Neoliberal Discourse from Data

Getting by

- Rejecting assistance
- Rejection of "struggling" or "poor"
- Proving yourself as independent
- Pride in accomplishments in poverty
- Self-identification as good economic managers

Natalie:	*I don't, in general, I will, I have never asked for money in terms of that … I get by as best I can.*
Teresa:	*I don't consider myself poor, financially. I manage to get by.*
Emily:	*I want to get myself together and I understand like the reasons … because life is easier in many ways.*

Hardworking/work ethic

- Reciting long work histories
- Talk on effortfulness (Gibson, 2009)
- Proud vs. "lost pride"
- Meritocracy talk
- Everyday poverty behaviour is hard work
- Working under health and economic constraints

Charlotte:	*So many people think that they have worked hard … everyone works hard.*
Teresa:	*I've had this work ethic, this work ethic has been there in my life.*
Sandra:	*It's hard work dealing with your own mind day in, day out.*
Donna:	*[Pay] rates were low … it's* ***hard bloody work,*** *working for 4 hours non-stop [with an injury], going back, it just exacerbated everything.*

Self-reliance/the other poor

- There are "different types or kinds of poor people"
- Drugs, alcohol, and poor education
- More skilled than those better off
- 'Others' are bad financial managers
- Welfare programmes are for 'others'

Sandra:	*You look at the ones with alcoholism and the one with drug problems … I mean the stuff is designed for the most … to assist those that are not at their brainiest.*
Michael:	*You know, it's like so many, it's unbelievable, I just go around, and I see people that can't even count … and I'm like* ***why am I unemployed?***
Adam:	*I always thought about it, I was pretty young when I realised how much money cigarettes cost … I don't know why, they get them … I always had an idea of the worth of a dollar whereas* ***you know*** *…*

well with so little and rejecting assistance, then an increase is unnecessary. Others did use these claims to challenge the deservingness of the poor. The pride in this talk too could promote a central claim of the neoliberal welfare policy; that striving alone is psychologically beneficial and preferable and, therefore, reductions in government assistance is beneficial (Mead, 1986; P. R. Saunders, 2004). Such outcomes are not intended by participants because they contradict efforts to increase benefits, reduce means-testing, and promote universal basic incomes as well as establish solidarity.

Solidarity Discourse

The solidarity building between poor people and the public was a palpable, constant, and acknowledged effort by everyone I spoke with. The function of solidarity was said to be resistance, but this came in nebulous forms. This set of repertoires allowed for frank discussion of stressful life events without being blamed, even protecting against scrutiny should someone forgo economic gain. Group, intergroup, and wider community solidarity and camaraderie ultimately promoted and encouraged cooperation and the sharing of goals.

Community Group

Sharing stories emphasised effortfulness in opposition to implications of bludging, snobbery, and laziness. Some challenged neoliberal values in conversations, while others shared their long work histories, or their many job applications and training sessions, but solidarity was in the "constant slog" providing them with almost nothing. Much of this talk came in the form of joking, though sometimes laced with sorrow and anger at the failure of the meritocracy or the death of Australia as 'the lucky country', the land of 'a fair go'. Events run by the group took up these caricatures, where centre pieces were humorous, dark, and scornful spins on colloquial phrases of Australian life drawing attention to the real experiences of poor people.

Stories also helped to justify behaviour, for example, the solidarity and encouragement around dumpster diving and anti-waste beliefs "it is something we have to do" (also see Vinegar et al., 2016, p. 249). Constant conversations about hope were made, though at events and organising meetings solidarity became a weapon, political agitation. Many group efforts were attempts to use relationships with political figures, service providers, and media to change what these groups did to them, or rather said about them. These groups had direct impacts on the everyday resources poor people would have access to.

Media

I was lucky to be part of passionate resistance against the degradation of the poor as a group. I lost track of the many horrible things said about the unemployed Australians and those in receipt of welfare, but they pushed back. The most worrying times in the group were the announcements of new punitive and restrictive welfare policies but these were times when solidarity could come to the fore.

Harmful media was a focusing lens for solidarity. Peel (2003, p. 34) mentioned a 'solidarity of outrage' when describing the stories shared by participants in Bidwill of a destructive riot, even if it was obvious the participants were not witnesses of the event. Similarly, in my research the highly educated group members, or those constantly engaged with news cycles, would share media, and speak at events rallying everyone against the images made of the poor. As people took on these arguments, rather than giving into the image or taking on the construct of dole bludger, the group was constantly sparking opposition. Most palpably were when the previously dejected and resigned members of the community were suddenly emboldened, telling me they felt like something could change even though they knew how hard and long a battle it would be. This culminated in growing attendance and continued voice both in media and in discussion with those in powerful positions.

Media that supported the fight was a particular delight to see. Sandra spoke about television shows and movies which helped her understand her responsibility as someone getting by, especially the movie *I, Daniel Blake*. This film was often mentioned in conversations. Putting the bleak situation of welfare provision in Britain on the screen for all to see, calling for change. The film resonated with members given the accuracy of the portrayal especially the horrid treatment by frontline workers wearing down welfare recipients.

Reactive Politics

Much of the group talk, and action, was reactive against government and media pressure.

Adam: *If it wasn't for [the group] I wouldn't know my rights, but I have always been … more reactive when something goes wrong. I will work out why it is, why that all happened and … it's why I reached out to the groups in the first place, but I always have been the person who when something happens that is not fair, I speak out against it.*

Emily: *We don't have a central place where we set the agenda. We are very reactive which is why we are always having to respond to things … because we are not in a position as a movement to say, "this is what we inevitably want down the road".*

Everyone was unified against those who imposed dispositional attributions and identities of failure onto the poor. Peel (2003, p. 136) also spoke of efforts to motivate the excluded to develop solidarity against an identifiable foe. Such efforts were not without complications.

Several participants described interpersonal and ideological conflicts between members. Some members resisted change in the group, others found new members too "gung-ho" for the groups benefit. Some people were "too aggressive". There were other disagreements from unsustainable exchanges.

Charlotte: *I think so in [the group] there has been a lot of people that kind of stretch themselves pretty thin and get burnt out and stuff and um I think a lot of people over commit to things*

Or disagreements on how the group should operate.

Natalie: *Then with these people a lot of people in [the group] seem to hate to know what is wrong with [other groups] but make the same mistakes. And they are just knocking people out with their actions and are nonplussed about it. "Get out with this idea and that one!"*

Who 'they' or 'them' are often blurred between real people and ideological positions. For example, multiple participants, while themselves aligned to the political left, spoke of 'them' as both the conservative, right-wing, aligned individuals but then also, those who did not action left-wing politics. Those who took on those ideological perspectives were labelled as 'them', even group members functionally as an insult. This was a worry for some of my participants.

Michael: *They all spill their guts on, and run themselves into the ground, and don't give a fuck when [supporters] disappear. It's just like, well that person was really awful, people do it all the time, and it's like where is the real enemy, you know? I just don't agree with it. I just say whatever I feel like ... I support the vast majority of like you know issues, like transgender whatever, but the way that a lot of them go about it it's just totally wrong. It's repeating the mistakes of the old socialist left again... It's just badgering.*

Criticism often would be identified as opposition, and by that fact support for neoliberal capitalism. Such verbal categorisation, 'with us or against us', did not just describe differences but enforced differentiation (see Phelan, 2014).

Similarly, the notions of ideology as political became contentious. There was discussion on when ejecting members was appropriate. As a rule, the group prohibited discrimination against gender and sexual minorities, racial groups, and religious minorities. Such a prohibition became problematic, for example, when members blamed their poverty, job redundancy, or disconnection from society on immigration. Similarly, there was a push against pairing antipoverty politics with climate change and gender politics. In some interviews and informal conversations, I was given Australia-first populism as a better solution to poverty than environmental protection or gender equality.

At other times the seclusion of the group, compared to the wider community, became a point of contention. Teresa, for example, reported wanting to allow the group to expand, and include those experiencing constraints while not appearing stereotypically poor.

Teresa: *There was a lady there ... she dresses rich like the mature, not matronly. Probably my age ... but she was wearing the white and the gold chain ... and her son, something happened, so she was trying to get him on a disability payment and she was talking about the frustrations ... [that] she was being impacted, and she didn't realise how hard it was ... that is the kind of person we need in the group ... to show that poverty doesn't just effect the stereotyped poor person ... It is people like her that will get the media attention, unfortunately.*

While indirect, other members, maintaining a vague notion of poverty, suggested not giving voice, time, or effort to those that were not poor, including women like Teresa describes, who were 'them'. The reason given was to avoid diluting the power of poor people's voices in a poor people's organisation.

The solidarity of the group was contingent on some, sometimes unforeseen, assumptions of the experience of poverty – generally an assumption of left-wing political alignment and, at minimum, leniency towards anti-capitalist talk (see Feagin, 1972). There were counterweights of concern that either there would be relaxation of antidiscrimination group rules, or that belief in strict rules would shun poor people who did not meet expectations. As members came and left the group, I noted these discursive struggles for solidarity linked to their burnout.

Mazelis (2017) participated with a welfare rights group and found mistrust. Participation seemed contingent on the available resources that the group could offer its members. The group in Mazelis' work controlled a limited number of public housing tickets but to be a recipient; there was an expectation of consistent participation. Sadly, in my research the community group had no tangible resources to provide, apart from being a network of weak ties with opportunities for small cash gigs (Granovetter, 1973). Otherwise accompanying someone to an appointment for advocacy was a possibility but only by a small handful of group members.

Durkheim (1933/2003; Cattell, 2001, p. 1502) distinguished between solidarity of traditional communities that could consistently exchange with each other producing a 'thick' trust, compared to modern 'organic' solidarity from fewer exchanges producing a 'thin' trust. My work and Mazelis's (2017) seem to describe the latter. There has been good argument against assuming solidarity, homogeneity, or harmony as defaults for such community groups (Collins, 2005, p. 14; Guijt & Kaul Shah, 1998; Norton, 1998; Wacquant, 2002). I suggest the expectation should be that without more resources to consistently exchange there will be disposability of relationships (Desmond, 2012) and discursive challenges that cannot be bridged without thicker trust.

Repertoires of Solidarity

There were several repertoires that participants drew on to establish and maintain their verbal position 'in solidarity' (Table 7.2). At times these were forceful and direct, in other cases, their use was just the everyday conversation in the group.

The focus on issues, on us versus them, and on failure of our systems, as forceful as these are, were exclusively part of relationship building and maintenance amongst the 'Us' group opposed to efforts to radically alter how others, such as politicians, media, and frontline workers, behave and spoke with poor people. These features are still challenges to dispositional attributions of poverty, like neoliberal repertoires. When speaking to others, 'them', publicly or in meetings a balance between solidarity and neoliberal discourses arose.

The Balancing Act

Tensions arise between these discourses and audiences. Unfortunately, adhering only to the solidarity discourse was difficult, and came to a head when resources were absent. The issues could not be resolved by the spoken strength of a relationship, nor by logic and argument, but rather if real and useful resources were available to keep the relationship going. Reproducing and behaving with neoliberal expectations worked better to get resources but could result in identification as 'them'. It is not surprising then that the cycles of burn out and disengagement seemed to be frequent not only for group participation but also for engagement with helping services and the welfare system in general.

Group members invoked an 'enough' or 'getting by' repertoire. They "had enough", and they were "doing well" despite struggling. It was enough to resist blame for their poverty. They were not lazy; they were utilising their resources as best they could. A narrative of striving against the odds allowed for pride in poverty. In other cases, recognising they are "okay", "comfortable", or "managing" resisted attributions of being "sad sacks" or someone that had "given up". Often people invoked "real poverty", absolute poverty which was "obviously" worse than their experience. The participants, then, are stuck between claiming the reality of their poverty while also arguing they are managing and doing well due to hard work with limited resources. Their pride in managing poverty cannot negate the shame of being poor; otherwise, they may lose the right to claim assistance.

TABLE 7.2 Repertoires for the Solidarity Discourse from Data

Structural fault

- External attribution and locus of control
- Systematic punitive systems
- Fragmented and uncaring institutional power (strangers)
- Extreme effort required to get out of poverty
- Gendered and disability-based structural issues
- Intentional system

Sandra:	*I mean the electricity system is the same. They have absolutely no compassionate bones in their body at all.*
Eden:	*No interface between the welfare and privatised systems.*
Sandra:	*Not at all, not at all.*
Charlotte:	*There is this huge misunderstanding from people who aren't in poverty. People expect that you can either do both, you can work yourself out of it and then they are like "Why don't you go out much" and it's like maybe because I have to work double the hours you do to get what you do and then I don't have time to go down to the pub with you! … everyone expects you to turn out fine.*
Emily:	*For me [care + study + work] reinforced where I am at and reinforced the structural imbalance. It's the norm now for people to say "I can do this" here "I will do this" there, and that is awful … Seeing the counsellor and she is like "What you are doing is like way too much" … but at the same time the world is unforgiving.*
Michael:	*Yeah, but they go "Oh, this is a shit time". It's supposed to be, you should feel bad about being on Centrelink.*

Us vs. Them

- Vague categories, often reactive
- "Them" included 'other' poor people denying poverty experiences
- "We know what it is like, they do not know what it is like"
- "We have it harder, they have it easier"
- Service providers could be "us" or "them"
  - Most did not understand and were "them"
- Government did not understand and were "them"
- Advocating and teaching rights

Charlotte:	*Oh yeah it can [cause] conflicts with them. Arguing with them and stuff. It doesn't really conflict with other ideals I've got from family members. I tend to just see them in a different way. Like "working hard for what you have got"; I believe in that, and they believe in that. We just might not see what working hard means and how hard the poor people are working compared to some of the people who have a lot more.*
Adam:	*One of my friends … he works in his dad's business as you would expect … so he doesn't actually realise how well he has got it. I was like "Get your dad to let me work there" I have more chance on that than anything.*
Sandra:	*What a lot of government officials don't get is, and it's what a lot of people don't get; it's a ripple effect and it continues and is why you have a continual pattern with people from lower socioeconomic areas because there is no other way to change it unless* ***you*** *are helping them change it, unless you are actually physically putting the help into helping them change it. [Then] it's never going to change.*

TABLE 7.2 (Continued)

Hope, coming together, and action	
Action as part of discourse is much less direct (field notes, no quotes) • 'Grand narratives', organisational stories, and organisation (meeting talk, etc.) • Political conversation and debate	• Encouraging cooperation and sharing – rejecting money • Outreach and community conversations for change (flyers) • Inspiring and speaking of hope (Sandra)

Participants recounted multiple times when the stress that came with interacting with others became too burdensome. Despite hating when others do it, Teresa avoided services and taking offered resources which "someone else will use". Charlotte said after she quit her job, she would avoid taking welfare payments and therefore Centrelink. Donna was reluctant to engage with the National Disability Insurance Scheme (NDIS) out of fear it could trigger reviews of her disability status. Living in fear of sudden status changes was constant in the group (also Garthwaite, 2014). These types of worries are hard to overcome.

The poor have goals set for them, to be self-reliant, to strive alone, to work on themselves. Attempts to rebut these claims were often attempts to show they were already self-reliant and striving. In turn, they limited their right to claim further assistance; asking for more assistance negates their self-reliance. This tension seemed to appear every time someone offered something for free in the group. Group members would evoke the 'enough' or 'getting by' repertoire and then reject assistance. They 'were good at managing money' and, therefore, any help would be taking more than needed.

The more the participants disengage, avoid resources, and limit their service use, the more they are confirmed as hardworking, independent, and self-reliant. Just as the group attempts to agitate and antagonise 'them' to change their behaviour, the welfare system is doing the same to the poor. Unfortunately, the poor do not control the flow of resource and efforts of the group spiral down, depleting resources, leading to social isolation and burnout.

Simmel (1908/1965, p. 121) said:

> We will see, on the contrary, that when assistance to the poor derives teleologically from a goal one hopes to pursue in this way, rather than from the causal basis of a real and effective unity among all the members of the group, the rights of the poor dwindle to nothingness.

There is a feedback loop, but not in the poor's cognition, it is in the discursive and contextual practice of support – urging the poor to be independently successful while churning in poverty. The very push towards independence maintains their poverty.

Simultaneously the members spoke invoked the phantom group of poor people that *do* need that assistance. Members claimed their efforts were directed towards this worse off group, while denying assistance, food baskets, or help and maintaining their poverty. Being a 'good' poor person means maintaining your poverty.

The balancing act occurs when arguing for policy change as well. The group consistently spoke about reports like a Deloitte Access Economics report (2018) which suggested a four billion dollar "prosperity dividend" would be generated nationally if unemployment benefits were raised by $75 a week. Such arguments are balanced on the idea that such a raise would help private businesses and the market. Advocating and argument for market benefits happened simultaneously with the group arguing against free-market solutions and capitalist rhetoric.

This issue culminated in appeals to the private market and neoliberal ideology for assistance to the poor. It is problematic, and confusing, to understand the balancing act as one that almost always simultaneously agrees with and defies ideological positions. As discourse, however, the idea of agreeing or disagreeing becomes temporary and functional. What is clear is without more, or 'thicker', solidarity the promotion of the neoliberal argument will win out every time, and the political outcomes, as disheartening as some were, will continue.

Eden: *But we cannot survive these guys?*
Donna: *No. No! Look at welfare, countries with a welfare state, we used to be up there now we are down, down in the low, 20th or something, privatising everything, hospitals next …*

Balancing acts, called 'double acts', or 'double shuffles', have been seen before. In the UK the New Labour policies, 'the third way' in the early 2000s, aimed to be both neoliberal and socially democratic. The double act produced only neoliberal outcomes (Levitas, 2005, p. 234). The balancing act cannot be sustained when capital, income, and material goods are the focus of research and policy while the 'social element' is absent (Levitas, 2005, p. xi).

There are some strictly psychological implications of the balancing act. Purpose and stability are, apparently, possible if the poor give up the happiness now, and then potentially, paradoxically, they could gain it back later? In my work, a mother was told to take minimum wage jobs, starting at 7 am that will "set her up for the future" and delay the gratification of being with her children for their morning meal. An educated person should take a job without passion, to "make good" (Orwell, 1936/2000). A disabled person should be happy with passivity to maintain their claim to a pension. For me, as someone that read all I could from economics and psychology, I cannot help but think better financial literacy or improved willpower to delay gratification would help but at huge costs. No one intends this to be the suggestion, but these are the options. Reintroducing the social relational exchanges show that poverty is brought about by everyone else more than 'the poor' themselves.

Everyone is complicit in the discursive construction of poverty. The antagonism this balancing act displays can appear even in friendly relationships, such as with friends and family that hold different political views, or loving relationships with those that are well-off (Laclau & Mouffe, 2001 in Phelan, 2014, p. 47). This antagonism appeared by group members intending to be benevolent. Members with know-how, intelligence, education, or simply, kindness, who go out of their way to give more to others than they take themselves. But in my work, I never spoke to someone in this other group – this phantom poor person who *really* needed help.

The poor must be the best effective managers of all things economic, helping some phantom group of poor people, while also existing in the reality of poverty. If any one of these ways of talking about the situation is relinquished, hope to have demands heard by the powerful becomes an infinitely more complex discursive battle. This same structure, of two conflicting discourses and the reality of poverty and deprivation, are used by the powerful strangers to limit and add obligations, sanctions, and monitoring to assistance.

Why Blame Everyone?

Unfortunately, the reason for the poor to display themselves in a good light, as effortful, hardworking, independent, and separate from the deviant, is how we get bad media images of the poor. Wacquant (2002, pp. 1469, 1527), when reviewing ethnographies of the poor, describes this issue for academics as "exoterism" with "sentimentalism", which "sanitises" or "glamorises" the participants' stories making them into "paragons of morality". Wacquant presents a critical articulation of an issue many in the field contend with. Recounting descriptions given by participants is paired with admiration and praise. No doubt distasteful features are removed to glamorise or sanitise the experiences. Further, it seems that everyone wishes to avoid the systemic and cyclical elements of poverty that implicate the poor in the very problems they face. I am trying to avoid sanitation or glamorisation, while trying to make clear it is not a choice to take part in these ways of talking, rather it is forced upon poor people.

The experiences I saw and heard were reasonable and human. Sometimes the group members were mean or petty, sometimes they were aware and apologised, sometimes they defended themselves, sometimes they constructed narratives to justify their actions. At other times they were polite, kind, and altruistic, but these extremes were rarer than the everyday neutral, tired, and generally worn-down context of what they face every day. My field notes had cases that are problematic to include, I, by no means, avoid moralistic sanitisation. Sometimes the behaviours were destructive and egoistic, with no amount of contextualisation excusing the effects on others; sometimes, in fact, contextualisation can accentuate how horrible poor people can be to one another. Not including these stories helps resist a psychological reduction implying poor people are just victims of their 'free personal choice'. I want to present people with a reasonable range of emotion, expression, and judgement, sometimes just and kind, sometimes egoistic and harmful.

Researchers, therefore, while justified in their call for 'better' images and discourses of the poor, must be wary of the outcomes. The images produced are not neutral and indeed can be reformulated to be used against the poor. Those who separate themselves from the deviant and pathological phantom group of poor people, those who shine with pride over their economic know-how to churn successfully, are the source of arguments that "poverty doesn't exist in developed nations" and could be evidence that going hungry and cold is just some perverse comfort or choice. Here, I suggest working to be a 'good poor person' comes with behaviours which maintain poverty. Structural forces paradoxically mandate refusing assistance to maintain the right to claim assistance. Breaking this cycle may mean being *a stereotypically bad poor person*. Research should be wary of producing only good images of poor people, and instead problematise who the bad images of the poor are for. Or better yet, start producing bad images of those who deprive, exclude, and constrain others by what they do and say even if that includes us as researchers, and the public – such agitation may expand the solidarity discourse.

Conclusions

At this point, there is little that can separate how people talk in social relationships from the resources they can exchange and manage through social relationships. The poor define their poverty in a myriad of ways. Most of these ways of talking about poverty are personal, and about the interconnections between resources, social relationships, and the pathways that are available. The ultimate fault here is expecting the issue to be found with poor people when the issue comes from interaction with everyone else.

Stressful life events are produced and are affected by how the poor talk about their poverty. The people they interact with, and the systems those people represent, consistently producing tension and worry. Even amongst the poor, as resources are depleted, or discursive conflict occurs, people dispose of relationships, avoid assistance, increase their poverty and deprivation, constrain social relationships, increase social exclusion and capabilities deprivation. These effects are cycles and processes, cycling up and down: *churning* (Hulme & Shepard, 2003).

References

Ali, S., Sensoy Bahar, O., Gopalan, P., Lukasiewicz, K., Parker, G., McKay, M., & Walker, R. (2018). "Feeling less than a second class citizen": Examining the emotional consequences of poverty in New York City. *Journal of Family Issues, 39*(10), 2781–2805. https://doi.org/10.1177/0192513X18760348

Archer, V. (2006). *In search of the Australian dole bludger constructing discourse of welfare 1974–83* [doctoral thesis]. Australian National University. https://openresearch-repository.anu.edu.au/handle/1885/9268

Archer, V. (2009). Dole bludgers, tax payers and the new right: Constructing discourses of welfare in 1970s Australia. *Labour History: A Journal of Labour and Social History*, (96), 177–190. doi:10.3828/27713750

Arthurson, K., & Jacobs, K. (2009). Discourses about Australian social housing, social exclusion and employment: Indications of the post-welfare state?. *Housing, Theory and Society, 26*(3), 179–192. doi:10.1080/14036090801939828

Bandelj, N. (2012). Relational work and economic sociology. *Politics & Society, 40*(2), 175–201. doi:10.1177/0032329212441597

Baum, F., & Duvnjak, A. (2013). The politics of poverty in Australia. *Social Alternatives, 32*(1), 12.

Broughton, C. (2003). Reforming poor women: The cultural politics and practices of welfare reform. *Qualitative Sociology, 26*(1), 35–51. https://doi.org/10.1023/A:1021451903511

Brown, L., Osborne, K., Walker, R., Moskos, M., Isherwood, L., Patel, K., ... & King, D. (2017). The benefits of a life-first employment program for Indigenous Australian families: Implications for 'Closing the Gap'. *Journal of Social Inclusion, 8*(1), 78–95, https://josi.journals.griffith.edu.au/index.php/inclusion/article/view/928/849

Cattell, V. (2001). Poor people, poor places, and poor health: The mediating role of social networks and social capital. *Social Science & Medicine (1982), 52*(10), 1501–1516. https://doi.org/10.1016/s0277-9536(00)00259-8

Chaufan, C., Constantino, S., & Davis, M. (2013). 'You must not confuse poverty with laziness': A case study on the power of discourse to reproduce diabetes inequalities. *International Journal of Health Services, 43*(1), 143–166. doi:http://dx.doi.org/10.2190/HS.43.1.j

Collins, S. B. (2005). An understanding of poverty from those who are poor. *Action Research, 3*(1), 9–31. doi:10.1177/1476750305047983

Cook, K. (2012). Neoliberalism, welfare policy and health: A qualitative meta-synthesis of single parents' experience of the transition from welfare to work. *Health, 16*(5), 507–530. doi:10.1177/1363459311434650

Coser, L. (1965). The sociology of poverty: To the memory of Georg Simmel. *Social Problems, 13*(2), 140–148. doi:10.2307/798899

Dean, H. (2003). Discursive repertoires and the negotiation of well-being: Reflections on the WeD frameworks. ESRC Research Group on *Wellbeing in developing countries Working Paper 4*. Available from http://citeseerx.ist.psu.edu/viewdoc/download?doi=10.1.1.476.2945&rep=reTeresa&type=pdf

Deeming, C., & Smyth, P. (2015). Social investment after neoliberalism: Policy paradigms and political platforms. *Journal of Social Policy, 44*(2), 297–318. doi:https://doi.org/10.1017/S0047279414000828

Deloitte Access Economics. (2018). Analysis of the impact of raising benefit rates. Australian Council of Social Service. Available from www.acoss.org.au/wp-content/uploads/2018/09/DAE-Analysis-of-the-impact-of-raising-benefit-rates-FINAL-4-September-...-1.pdf

Dodson, L. (2013). Stereotyping low-wage mothers who have work and family conflicts. *Journal of Social Issues, 69*(2), 257–278. https://doi.org/10.1111/josi.12014

Durkheim, E. (1933/2003). *Division of labour in society*. Free Press.

Desmond, M. (2012). Disposable ties and the urban poor. *American Journal of Sociology, 117*(5), 1295–1335. https://doi.org/10.1086/663574

Engels, B. (2006). Old problem, new label: Reconstructing the problem of welfare dependency in Australian social policy discourse. *Just Policy: A Journal of Australian Social Policy*, (41), 5–14.

Fairclough, N. (2002). Language in new capitalism. *Discourse & Society, 13*(2), 163–166. doi:10.1177/0957926502013002404

Fairclough, N. (2004). *Analysing discourse textual analysis for social research*. Routledge.

Farrell, L. C., Warin, M. J., Moore, V. M., & Street, J. M. (2016). Socio-economic divergence in public opinions about preventive obesity regulations: Is the purpose to 'make some things cheaper, more affordable' or to 'help them get over their own ignorance'?. *Social Science & Medicine, 154*, 1–8. https://doi.org/10.1016/j.socscimed.2016.02.028

Feagin, J. R. (1972). Poverty: We still believe that God helps those who help themselves. *Psychology Today, 6*(6), 101–110.

Garthwaite, K. (2014). Fear of the brown envelope: Exploring welfare reform with long-term sickness benefits recipients. *Social Policy & Administration, 48*(7), 782–798. doi:10.1111/spol.12049

Garthwaite, K. A., Collins, P. J., & Bambra, C. (2015). Food for thought: An ethnographic study of negotiating ill health and food insecurity in a UK foodbank. *Social Science & Medicine, 132*, 38–44. http://dx.doi.org/10.1016/j.socscimed.2015.03.019

Gazso, A. (2007). Balancing expectations for employability and family responsibilities while on social assistance: Low-income mothers' experiences in three Canadian provinces. *Family Relations, 56*(5), 454–466. www.jstor.org/stable/4541688

Gibson, S. (2009). The effortful citizen: Discursive social psychology and welfare reform. *Journal of Community & Applied Social Psychology, 19*(6), 393–410. DOI: 10.1002/casp.1003

Gibson, S. (2011). Dilemmas of citizenship: Young people's conceptions of un/employment rights and responsibilities. *British Journal of Social Psychology, 50*(3), 450–468. doi:10.1348/014466610X520113

Godfrey, E. B., & Wolf, S. (2016). Developing critical consciousness or justifying the system? A qualitative analysis of attributions for poverty and wealth among low-income racial/ethnic minority and immigrant women. *Cultural Diversity and Ethnic Minority Psychology, 22*(1), 93. http://dx.doi.org/10.1037/cdp0000048

Grahame, T., & Marston, G. (2012). Welfare-to-work policies and the experience of employed single mothers on income support in Australia: Where are the benefits?. *Australian Social Work, 65*(1), 73–86. http://dx.doi.org/10.1080/0312407X.2011.604093

Granovetter, M. S. (1973). The strength of weak ties. *American Journal of Sociology, 78*(6), 1360–1380. www.jstor.org/stable/2776392

Guerin, B. (2015). *How to rethink psychology: New metaphors for understanding people and their behavior*. Routledge.

Guerin, B. (2016). *How to rethink human behavior: A practical guide to social contextual analysis*. Routledge.

Guerin, B., Leugi, G. B., & Thain, A. (2018). Attempting to overcome problems shared by both qualitative and quantitative methodologies: Two hybrid procedures to encourage diverse research. *The Australian Community Psychologist, 29*(2), 74.

Guerin, B., & Wood, E. (2017). Why do adolescents lie in the sun when they know it is risky? Contextualizing the 'attitude-behavior' gap and the 'optimistic bias' as verbal behaviour. *Educere et Educare: Revista de Educação, 13*, 1–15.

Guijt, I., & Kaul Shah, M. (1998). Waking up to power, conflict and process. In I. Guijt & M. Kaul Shah (eds.), *The myth of community: Gender issues in participatory development* (pp. 1–23). Intermediate Technology Publications.

Harper, D. J. (1996). Accounting for poverty: From attribution to discourse. *Journal of Community & Applied Social Psychology, 6*(4), 249–265. https://doi.org/10.1002/(SICI)1099-1298(199610)6:4<249::AID-CASAdam69>3.0.CO;2-U

Hulme, D., & Shepherd, A. (2003). Conceptualizing chronic poverty. *World Development, 31*(3), 403–423. doi:10.1016/S0305-750X(02)00222-X

Jette, S., & Rail, G. (2014). Resisting, reproducing, resigned? Low-income pregnant women's discursive constructions and experiences of health and weight gain. *Nursing Inquiry, 21*(3), 202–211. https://doi.org/10.1111/nin.12052

Laclau, E., & Mouffe, C. (2001). *Hegemony and socialist strategy*. Verso.

Levitas, R. (2005). *The inclusive society?: Social exclusion and new labour*. Springer.

MacDonald, R., & Marsh, J. (2005). *Disconnected youth? Growing up in Britain's poor neighbourhoods*. Palgrave Macmillan. https://doi.org/10.1057/9780230511750

Marston, G. (2008). A war on the poor: Constructing welfare and work in the twenty-first century. *Critical Discourse Studies, 5*(4), 359–370. https://doi.org/10.1080/17405900802405312

Marston, G., & McDonald, C. (2007). Assessing the policy trajectory of welfare reform in Australia. *Benefits, 15*(3), 233–245.

Mason, C., Spinks, A., Hajkowicz, S., & Hobman, L. (2014). Exploring the contribution of frontline welfare service delivery to capability development in Australia. *Journal of Social Policy, 43*(3), 635–653.

Mazelis, J. M. (2015). "I got to try to give back": How reciprocity norms in a poor people's organization influence members' social capital. *Journal of Poverty, 19*(1), 109–131. https://doi.org/10.1080/10875549.2014.979458

Mazelis, J. M. (2017). *Surviving poverty: Creating sustainable ties among the poor*. NYU Press.

Mead, L. M. (1986). *Beyond entitlement: The social obligations of citizenship*. Free Press.

Norton, A. (1998). Analysing participatory research for policy change. In J. Holland & J. Blackburn (eds.), *Whose voice? Participatory research and policy change* (pp. 179–191). Intermediate Technology Publications.

Orwell, G. (1936/2000). *Keep the aspidistra flying*. Penguin UK.

Palmer, C., Ziersch, A., Arthurson, K., & Baum, F. (2004). Challenging the stigma of public housing: Preliminary findings from a qualitative study in South Australia. *Urban Policy and Research*, *22*(4), 411–426. doi: 10.1080/0811114042000296326

Parker, I. (2002). *Critical discursive psychology*. Palgrave MacMillan.

Patrick, R. (2016). Living with and responding to the 'scrounger' narrative in the UK: Exploring everyday strategies of acceptance, resistance and deflection. *Journal of Poverty and Social Justice*, *24*(3), 245–259. doi:10.1332/175982716X14721954314887

Peel, M. (2003). *The lowest rung: Voices of Australian poverty*. Cambridge University Press.

Pemberton, S., Fahmy, E., Sutton, E., & Bell, K. (2016). Navigating the stigmatised identities of poverty in austere times: Resisting and responding to narratives of personal failure. *Critical Social Policy*, *36*(1), 21–37. DOI: 10.1177/0261018315601799

Phelan, S. (2014). *Neoliberalism, media and the political*. Springer.

Potter, J., & Wetherell, M. (1987). *Discourse and social psychology: Beyond attitudes and behaviour*. Sage.

Pulkingham, J., Fuller, S., & Kershaw, P. (2010). Lone motherhood, welfare reform and active citizen subjectivity. *Critical Social Policy*, *30*(2), 267–291. https://doi.org/10.1177/0261018309358292

Reid, C., & Tom, A. (2006). Poor women's discourses of legitimacy, poverty, and health. *Gender & Society*, *20*(3), 402–421. doi:10.1177/0891243206286939

Saunders, P. R. (2004). *Australia's welfare habit and how to kick it*. Duffy & Snellgrove Centre for Independent Studies.

Shildrick, T., & MacDonald, R. (2013). Poverty talk: How people experiencing poverty deny their poverty and why they blame 'the poor'. *The Sociological Review*, *61*(2), 285–303. doi:10.1111/1467-954X.12018

Simmel, G. (1908/1965) The poor (C. Jacobson, Trans.). *Social Problems*, *13*(2), 118–140.

Springer, S. (2012). Neoliberalism as discourse: Between Foucauldian political economy and Marxian poststructuralism. *Critical Discourse Studies*, *9*(2), 133–147. https://doi.org/10.1080/17405904.2012.656375

Stahl, G., & Habib, S. (2017). Moving beyond the confines of the local: Working-class students' conceptualizations of belonging and respectability. *Young*, *25*(3), 268–285. doi:10.1177/1103308816669451

Strier, R., Eisikovits, Z., Sigad, L., & Buchbinder, E. (2016). Working men views of poverty: Ethnic perspectives. *Men and Masculinities*, *19*(5), 480–502. doi:10.1177/1097184X15613829

Townsend, P. (1979). *Poverty in the United Kingdom: A survey of household resources and standards of living*. University of California Press.

Verdouw, J. J. (2017). The subject who thinks economically? Comparative money subjectivities in neoliberal context. *Journal of Sociology*, *53*(3), 523–540. doi:10.1177/1440783316662717

Vinegar, R., Parker, P., & McCourt, G. (2016). More than a response to food insecurity: Demographics and social networks of urban dumpster divers. *Local Environment*, *21*(2), 241–253. doi:10.1080/13549839.2014.943708

Wacquant, L. (2002). Scrutinizing the street: Poverty, morality, and the pitfalls of urban ethnography. *American Journal of Sociology, 107*(6), 1468–1532. https://doi.org/10.1086/340461

Woodward, K. (2008). The multiple meanings of work for welfare-reliant women. *Qualitative Sociology, 31*(2), 149–168. doi:10.1007/s11133-008-9091-3

Zelizer, V. A. (2010). *Economic lives: How culture shapes the economy*. Princeton University Press.

8

WHY WE HAVE NOT SOLVED POVERTY

Given all these findings, and the tenacity of these findings, it seems so odd to me that the answer, solution, fix to poverty has not been implemented. Give people more, reward their every effort even if it is just getting up in the day. That fits with psych 101, that fits with the on-the-ground efforts of others, and while it is not my area, I am rather sure it fits with everyone's morals if the outcome is happier, healthier, and potentially economically well-off society. This book is laden with the major issues of the field: the rediscovery of old news, but more importantly the issues continue because I, like everyone else in society, choose to speak to, look at, and examine the lives of poor people to discover the cause and solution to poverty.

The Issue of Rediscovery

The behavioural and emotional content of my findings did not diverge too greatly from previous qualitative work in similar contexts. I can be happy that I put these in their unique contexts, blending the use of language with the experience of poverty. Previous research seems to treat contexts as enclosed – places where the findings happened – I would like to think you can see how you and the rest of society are interconnected through these contexts, that you are part of the findings. Ultimately reinforcing previous findings is not a strength of my work but also it is not really a failing – I am on the same track we all have been on for a while. The bigger question is why we keep just rediscovering these issues.

Potentially rediscovery is a result of academic mechanisms. As a PhD student I used previous literature as a springboard. Not a mistake or problem, but potentially it makes what is already known so much clearer and easier

DOI: 10.4324/9781003453970-8

to report. The other problem is that writing about these issues are part of globalised resistance discourses or, simply put, common ways of speaking about the experiences that may be reinforced because they function in many contexts to protect the poor from criticism. Will participants ever not use communal stories to describe their world? Probably not. What else do we have?

The issue of rediscovery signals the need for interdisciplinary research (Carr, 2013). Most of what I draw on is not psychological which made my work unique in its context – a school of psychology – but depending on who you are this may all seem obvious as it is in the literature you read all the time. But working together across fields, departments, and universities is so much easier said than done. Issues arise when disciplines try to maintain their identity by demarcating their concepts, theories, and areas of study. Psychology is constantly creating internal concepts to explain behaviour as even when to other disciplines contextual provides a simpler explanation. A potential solution is more *a-disciplinary* research, which seeks to incorporate all social science (Guerin, 2015, 2016). But the road between there and here is longer than I can suggest. At the least, my rediscovery makes it questionable for findings to be considered 'only psychological', as context made psychological claims making less and less sense as I got through my PhD.

Speaking Directly with Poor People

Choosing to speak to poor people was obviously a correct choice to understand what the issues they face are, but we have been rediscovering these for so long. There are so many other people relationally involved in this who were not the target but should be the target for change, as opposed to poor people themselves. Landlords, employers, frontline workers, the public, politicians, academics are all better targets for intervention if we want to help the poor in Australia.

There is also an issue of the volume of data. I spent so long with such a small number of people that a 60,000-word book ultimately presents a tiny sliver of their experiences while simultaneously being a tiny sample. Undoubtably, more time with participants would allow more to be learned from them; more participants reveal more pathways and more about some, now well-known, contexts. But more of the same is not validation of the claims for qualitative investigations. I now barely believe there is a uniform element that really unifies these people. On the contrary, it is the struggle against difference and differentiation that I found to be most problematic in the relational work. If you were to interact with someone experiencing poverty you cannot implicitly use any of this information as truth of their experience. This should be intimately true for clinical professionals like psychologists that read this book. On the other hand, you have trends, contexts, experiences, and ways of talking to observe for, and to try to explain when they are present and absent. Each person has their own massive volume of contexts, pathways, and behaviours. While transferable the notion of any generalisation from this work is antithetical to what I have described.

Another confusing point, that I am not settled on is the focus on interview data. At first the field notes revealed there was enough to analyse several important community contexts. The initial aims, the lack of notes on the digital participation, and the limited ability to ascribe consent to those at group events for what was shared, however, led to the decision that a more ethnographic analysis of the community group was not appropriate. These community contexts impacted on the lives of participants and may have application in community or the wider social context, but these points nonetheless could not reliably be described in the previous chapters unless they appeared in recorded conversations. The initial proposals for this research considered action research, but ultimately conversational research was decided upon. Future research should seek to incorporate as much of conversational research methods and action research as possible as the two seem compatible, but the time and intensity increase would not have been appropriate for a PhD project.

Finally, an important question hangs over the research. Is it still imperative to interview poor people to learn about poverty? Throughout the analysis process, the answer that stuck with me is: No. The rediscovery of similar findings, and my presentation, though anonymised and generalised, raised ethical and analytical questions. Even as an 'insider' to the experiences, talking to poor people for a PhD, data, and a book are positive functions of poverty. Equally not publishing all this effort to share stories would be wrong. This again is the finding that social relationships should be central to investigating poverty and that others have a large role to play in the everyday (re-)production of behavioural constraints.

Some of the above points could be solved by more researchers and more time. But as Peel (2003, p. 76) said:

> When your funding demands evidence of dramatic need and proof of efficient outcomes there is little to be gained by talking about chronic suffering and hopelessness and the long haul. What counts, after all, is the extent to which the poor have suffered and proven their endurance. In any event, your funding submission will have to boil down to five dot points, an executive summary and an outcome that can be measured. Nowhere are you invited to describe the complexity of poverty, or the problems that only make sense if you know something about hardship.

Until we as researchers address these complications for the economic context of carrying out research, it would be odd to expect future projects to be able to truly assist in the economic contexts of other people's whole lives.

Ways Forward for Research

One way forward then is to contextualise both sides of the exchanges and pathways. This presents a problem in that as researchers we would need to interview many more people to map contexts and pay close attention to discourse. A possible solution to this is to relinquish power of the conversational research to the participants, allowing them to record conversations with the important people in their life. Putting power in the hands of participants can be successful (e.g., Radley et al., 2005). Continuing this may also produce more frank and straightforward conversation, overcoming insider–outsider, 'monitorability', and relationship building interruptions. Participants will need and be able to have a part in the analysis process as well. The researcher's role of applying their special talents and educational privilege to add something to the analysis becomes even more important and may combat the critique that all qualitative research is, is curating small illustrative quotes (Thain, 2023). This way forward draws the attention of poverty research and solutions away from the poor and into the contexts and pathways which are problematic, stressful, and constrained.

Further questions for research arose during the analysis process.

- What are the origins of discursive patterns used by participants and strangers?
- To what extent would people admit awareness or use of disposable relationships?
- What would qualitative investigations find for interventions in everyday human life such as obligation free cash transfers as has already been done quantitatively (e.g., Alves et al., 2019; Haushofer & Shaprio, 2016)?

Similar methods can be employed to address these questions but may require more pointed analysis and will almost certainly require the inclusion of social media and policy coverage found in online spaces.

Finally, research dedicated to generating intervention points, and strategies, or addressing blocks to new discursive repertoires on poverty are needed. But again, this is a rediscovery as Peel (2003, pp. 174–177) said:

> If most people aren't talking about injustice, inequality or poverty at the beginning of the twenty-first century, I don't think the problem is their hard-hearted incapacity to be moved. It is more complicated. Views are inconsistent, jarring, even contradictory. If there is an absence, it is of sensible discussion. The major political parties seem convinced that we ordinary voters are resolutely selfish, so they have trapped each other in a lacklustre debate about self-interest, lower taxes and the need to police welfare beneficiaries. Too many commentators are caught in the same tangle of 'spin' and bullyboy rhetoric. The failures have occurred at the

peak of power in Australia, particularly among people who have mistaken ordinary citizens' dislike of politics and rhetoric for a dislike of government and ideas.

We should use the above points, and the above suggestion to participant-controlled conversations, to address the ways in which the general Australian citizen is talking about the issues of poverty and policy, then we may be preventing some of the stress and protecting well-being.

Ways Forward for Intervention

Working with people directly reveals pathways full of constraints. Revealing these even on the individual level does a lot to fulfil the question of "what is the point" of knowing about poverty. As Orshansky says, it is "to do something about [it]" (1969, p. 37).

The Need for Social Relationships of Opportunity

There is a lack of, and need for, more positive social relationship between 'the poor' and the others in their resource–relationship pathways. This is particularly true of the strangers who represent institutions. I consistently heard about stranger relationships which were found to be lacking, or downright harmful including welfare bureaucracy workers, mental health workers, medical workers, and even the services directed at assisting the poor. These types of claims are well-worn, for example the efforts to analyse and evaluate the frontline worker bureaucracy (Lipsky, 1980/2010). Particularly problematic were the ways in which these people spoke which implied wrongdoing or a lack of self-responsibility on the part of the poor.

Relational studies consistently suggest intervention should involve a forceful reassessment of these relationships on a policy and legal level. For many participants the psychological effects from their accommodation were mediated by its social contexts. Those who lived with housemates or landlords they could trust or had good relationships with were generally positive (Michael, Emily) while those, the majority, who relied on strangers, who did not understand the context or constraints of poverty, behaved in a way that harmed their tenants (Teresa, Natalie, Donna). Stranger-based exchanges of money (rent) are the norm, but the group often spoke about landlords not understanding the social and cultural contexts and needs of their tenants. The group often advocated for more policy-based rights, but there is an argument for professionals to assist in larger social–cultural changes of how Australians view their responsibilities to each other as citizens when engaging in these often-decontextualised money-stranger exchanges.

One potential intervention is to address these ways of talking transparently and find ways as professionals to include agitation on these powerful stranger relationships directly in our work, for example, to be present in welfare offices to point out the problematic and disempowering discursive practices of workers. Participants often wanted to hold these strangers to account but did not have the power to do so, as resources only flowed from the stranger to the welfare recipient and power comes with control over resources.

That said, power being placed into the hands of professionals does not empower disadvantaged people. To create a context in which poor people can have greater effect with their words, when trying to control their resources, they would need contextual power – as context is the driving force behind functions of discourse (Guerin, 2016). One solution, often joked about in the anti-poverty group, was that evaluations of job network agencies, or Centrelink, should be in the hands of the disadvantaged themselves. The disadvantaged people should be trusted to be right more often than we may think (Peel, 2003). We should also be prepared that the heterogeneous group made up of 'poor people' will demand different outcomes of services, with different psycho-social and emotive qualities about them. Some participants showed a fondness for people that were direct and assertive, while others were focused on a hands-off approach that allowed flexibility.

Again, for poor people to have power in these situations they need command over their pathways. One possibility is to allow their voices and judgement to carry more weight in the funding for services – opposed to the current rating system based on employment outcomes alone, or the one off, short, testimony at inquests and meet and greets with politicians. This obviously would be a massive change from a strict economic and labour performance model to one that focuses on well-being, sociability between workers and clients, and redressing the relational components between the socio-economic groups of the country.

The Need for More Resources, Particularly More Money

The other clear and often advocated position is to reduce the obligations for welfare recipients outright. The group advocated for a raise to Newstart, but ultimately many saw a universal basic income as the better solution to their money problems. This type of change would disrupt the common neoliberal discourses on the poor, given that all Australians would be in receipt of this assistance and, therefore, labelling UBI recipients *dole bludgers* would include too many in the population to be a sustainable thing to say without challenge.

Unfortunately, these two suggestions are just as much rediscoveries as any other suggestions. Coser (1965) highlighted how Simmel believed the poor were demarcated by the request for assistance; therefore, removing the need for the request could remove the poor marker on people. At present assistance is only rendered after means testing and many mutual obligations are completed. Ronald Henderson in the (1975) government inquest into poverty suggested a 'guaranteed income scheme' paid to all Australians to keep them out of poverty regardless of the stability or instability of their income (pp. 67–87). So, Australian scholars at the forefront of poverty research, like Henderson, have long argued that without an increase in the poor's basic resources little can change. My insights are rediscoveries but also a note that money as a resource only functions through pathways with social relationships, and the discourses that mediate them. Just as without more resources, little will change if there is no change in the social–cultural, and psycho-social (emotive) lives of the poor.

So, for both research and intervention, psychology along with the other social sciences should focus on the other people in the pathways of poverty rather than the poor themselves. But again, I have rediscovered something: "One would like on the part of the psychologist a reversal of allegiance so that he [sic] endeavors to bring about a change in people who control the material resources of the world" (Mehryar, 1984, p. 166).

Final Comment

Poverty, not having enough, has been around for a long time. The hope in research like this is that one day we will live in a world where no one goes without, and no one feels "tightly wrapped", constrained, and lacking freedom. Tensions still exist between researchers and the participants in these types of studies, as researchers are usually more powerful, with more opportunities, and generally better off. At several points in this research, it felt like being on a treadmill – that research will continue to uncover the same core problems, and the same possible solutions, only to find, again, the slim chance of such programmes, policy, or assistance producing socio-cultural or psychological changes.

More can be done, and more should be done, but importantly, contexts keep changing. The content of this book was really finalised just as the pandemic hit and queues wrapped around local Centrelink offices and down the street. In a perverse way, this was positive as many more Australians were seeing the problems, worries, and constraints that the most disadvantaged Australians live with every day. As time goes on, we can hope, and work towards, not only understanding poverty personally and as professionals but also to encourage many others to get close to and learn from these experiences. As people come together to defend themselves against these shocks, as the community group does, hopefully the shape of Australian disadvantage changes and a focus on the psychological and social well-being in our community arise above the now well-worn financial fetishisation which pervades politics, psychological theories of poverty, and everyday lives of Australians.

There is an odd hope I feel from this work; that one day soon it will be useless; that we will fix this problem, and no one will be in poverty.

References

Alves, F. J. O., Machado, D. B., & Barreto, M. L. (2019). Effect of the Brazilian cash transfer programme on suicide rates: A longitudinal analysis of the Brazilian municipalities. *Social Psychiatry and Psychiatric Epidemiology, 54*(5), 599–606. https://doi.org/10.1007/s00127-018-1627-6

Carr, S. C. (2013). *Anti-poverty psychology*. Springer Science & Business Media.

Coser, L. (1965). The sociology of poverty: To the memory of Georg Simmel. *Social Problems, 13*(2), 140–148. doi:10.2307/798899

Guerin, B. (2015). *How to rethink psychology: New metaphors for understanding people and their behavior*. Routledge.

Guerin, B. (2016). *How to rethink human behavior: A practical guide to social contextual analysis*. Routledge.

Haushofer, J., & Shapiro, J. (2016). The short-term impact of unconditional cash transfers to the poor: Experimental evidence from Kenya. *The Quarterly Journal of Economics, 131*(4), 1973–2042. https://doi.org/10.1093/qje/qjw025

Henderson, R. J. A. (1975). *Australian government commission of inquiry into poverty*. Australian Government Publishing Service..

Lipsky, M. (1980/2010). *Street-level bureaucracy: Dilemmas of the individual in public service*. Russell Sage Foundation.

Mehryar, A. H. (1984). The role of psychology in national development: Wishful thinking and reality. *International Journal of Psychology, 19*(1–4), 159–167. https://doi.org/10.1080/00207598408247523

Orshansky, M. (1969). How poverty is measured. *Monthly Labor Review, 92*, 37.

Peel, M. (2003). *The lowest rung: Voices of Australian poverty*. Cambridge University Press.

Radley, A., Hodgetts, D., & Cullen, A. (2005). Visualizing homelessness: A study in photography and estrangement. *Journal of Community & Applied Social Psychology, 15*(4), 273–295. https://doi.org/10.1002/casp.825

Thain, E. (2023). "You think that, again, that's the medication": Reflecting on qualitative methods for interviewing family members of violent and impulsive men in an intervention trial. *Qualitative Research in Psychology, 20*(3), 471–501. https://doi.org/10.1080/14780887.2023.2240733

INDEX

Note: Page numbers in **bold** refer to tables.

abstraction 12, 71, 83, 84
agitation 129, 135, 138, 149
anthropology 24, 34, 48, 58
assumptions: discursive 83, 127, 132; economic 40–2; psychological 35, 36, 39–40, 122; poverty theory 22, 27, 52, 60, 62
attribution 34–6, 121, 130, 133, **134**
avoidance: discursive 57, 78, 82, 86–7, 132, 135; exchange 28, 58, 78, 85, 90–2; social **54**, 56, 88, 89

behavioural economics 40–2
belief 34–6, 38, 43, 48, 122, 127
bias 40–1
bludger 51, 121, 124, 126–7, 130, 149
bureaucracy: change 148; discourse 127; relationships 51–2, **53**, 56, 59, 83, **90**

capital 13, 17, 20, 25, 71, 78; discursive 131–3; social/cultural 20, **55**, 55, 57
cheat 6, 51, 124
cognitive feedback loop 37–40, 62–3, 135–6
community 5–7, **16**, 19–20, 52, 72–4, **89**
complexity 18, 57, 58, 63, 122, 146
control 15, **16**, 62, 92, 135, 149–50; discursive 124, **134**; economics 42, 76, 90; psychological 33, 35, 37, 39, 42
criminal 39, 78, 83, 127, 137–8

DA (discourse analysis) 119–20; *see* other subcategories "discursive"
disability 14, **16**, **53**, 55, 63; experiences 80, **87**, 127, 132, **134**, 135
disadvantage 12–13, 38, 43, 51, 81, 149–50
disposition *see* attribution
disposability 59, 85, 133
double hermeneutic 28
dumpster dive 51, 60–1, 129

economic North 1, 14, 22
education: poverty context **16**, 50, **54–5**, 55–6; poverty experiences 73, 78–9, 84, **87**, 93–4
effort: discursive 123, 127, **128**, 129, 137; work 3, 4, 35, 49, 79, 85
employment: discursive 121–2, 136; impacts **16**, **19**, 56, 59, 62; precarious 15, 63, 88; services 2, 149; unemployment 2, 35–6, 49–50; work 12, **16**, 52, **54**, 72, 149
error 38–42, 84

family **53–4**, 56, 73, 76, 78, **89**
friendship **16**, 19, 51, **54**; discourse 137; losing 80, 92

frontline: context 52, 55, 57, 59; discourse 122–3, 127, 130, 145, 148; experience 80, 83, 88, **89**

gender **54–5**, 72, 81, 83, 92; discourse 122, **134**; men 51, 56, 61; politics 131; women 50, 56, 61–2
generalisation 74–6, 83, 122, 146
government 17, 22, 53, 78–9, **89**; discourse 126, 130, **134**

hedonist *see* pleasure
housing 25, 50, **53**, 60, 73, 81

identity 56–7, 59, 81, 121–4, 127, 145
interdisciplinary 34, 57, 145
irrational *see* rationality
isolation 63, 78, 83, 91, 128, 135

job *see* employment

Lewis, O. 34, 39
lonely *see* isolation

Marx, K. 11
mental health **54–6**, 59–60, 73, 83–4, **87**
mental illness: anxiety **53**, 59, 63, 83–4, 90–1; depression **53**, 73, 91
monitoring 2, 52, 58–9, 62, 90, 147
multidimensionality 14–15, **16**, **27**

narrative **55**, 119, 133, **135**, 137
neoliberalism 49–50, **53**; discourses of 120, 124, **125**, 127, **128**, 136

obligations 2–3, 49, 52, **53–4**, 149–50; experiences 78, 85, 137
Orshansky, M. 1, 12, 18, 148
Orwell, G. 136

parenting: discourse 120, 122, 136; mothers **53–5**, 56–57, 61, 63, 77, 81
partnership **54**, 63, 78, 83, **89**
pathways 71–2, 147–50
Peel, M. 49–51, 129, 130, 146, 147
personality 34–5, 38–40, 50
phantom poor 120–2, 136–9
pleasure 39, 90–1, 116, 125
poverty: absolute poverty 13–14, 22–3, **27**, 70, 115, 133; capabilities **16**, 21–3, **27**; deprivation **16**, 17–20, **27**, **54**; exclusion **16**, 20–1, 24–5, **27**, 59, 71; income poverty **16**, 17–18, 25, **27**, 62; relative poverty 13–14, 17, **27**, 70; subjective poverty **16**, 23–4, **27**, 34
psychologist 34, 36, 43, 83, 145, 150
psychology: cognitive 37–8; literature 58–60; reduction 34, 122, 124, 138; social 18, 25, 40
psychotherapy *see* therapy
punish 3, 49, **53**, 124
purpose 77–9, 84, **86**, 136

rationality 3–4, 37–8, 40–3, 56–7, 91
rediscovery 49, 144–6, 149–50
rejection 42, 91, 92, 102, **128**, 135
resources 3, 11–12, **54–5**, 70–1, 133, 149–50
reward 3, 38, 79, 99, 144
Robodebt 90, 126
rural 74
Ryan, W. 34

self-: control 37, 39, 42; esteem 59; responsibility 49, 120, 148; reliant 48, 124, 127, **128**, 136
Sen, A. 21–3
Smith, A. 16, 18
social contextual analysis 48, 70–2
social financial connectedness 62; *also see* pathways
sociology 48, 58
solidarity 77, 82, 129, 132–3, **134**
stability 20, 57, 62, 83, 87–91
stranger relationships 58–9, 71; discourses with 127, **134**, 137, 148–9; experiences of 83–4, 89–90
stress 37–40, 62–3, 88–92, 123–4, 138
Sunstein, C. 41

Thaler, R. 40–1
therapy 38
Townsend, P. 18–20, 22–3
traits *see* personality
transport 56, 60, 73, 85

Universal Basic Income (UBI) 1–2, 149–50
urban 58–60

virtual 90

work *see* employment

Taylor & Francis Group
an informa business

Taylor & Francis eBooks

www.taylorfrancis.com

A single destination for eBooks from Taylor & Francis with increased functionality and an improved user experience to meet the needs of our customers.

90,000+ eBooks of award-winning academic content in Humanities, Social Science, Science, Technology, Engineering, and Medical written by a global network of editors and authors.

TAYLOR & FRANCIS EBOOKS OFFERS:

- A streamlined experience for our library customers
- A single point of discovery for all of our eBook content
- Improved search and discovery of content at both book and chapter level

REQUEST A FREE TRIAL

support@taylorfrancis.com

Routledge
Taylor & Francis Group

CRC Press
Taylor & Francis Group

For Product Safety Concerns and Information please contact our EU representative GPSR@taylorandfrancis.com
Taylor & Francis Verlag GmbH, Kaufingerstraße 24, 80331 München, Germany

www.ingramcontent.com/pod-product-compliance
Ingram Content Group UK Ltd.
Pitfield, Milton Keynes, MK11 3LW, UK
UKHW020002200926
475702UK00015B/2422